Adjusting *Adversity*

How Claims Pros Conquer Worst Case Scenarios

To Wayne Gearhart — Best wishes in "adjusting adversity"! Best regards,

By Kevin M. Quinley, CPCU, AIC

Kevin Quinley 10/27/03

The
NATIONAL UNDERWRITER
Company
PROFESSIONAL PUBLISHING GROUP

P.O. Box 14367 • Cincinnati, Ohio 45250-0367
1-800-543-0874 • www.nationalunderwriter.com

This publication is designed to provide accurate and authoritative information in regard to the subject matter covered. It is sold with the understanding that the publisher is not engaged in rendering legal, accounting or other professional service. If legal advice or other expert assistance is required, the services of a competent professional person should be sought. Ñ From a Declaration of Principles jointly adopted by a Committee of the American Bar Association and a Committee of Publishers and Associations.

About the Author

Kevin M. Quinley is senior vice president, Risk Services, for MED-MARC Insurance Company, Chantilly, Virginia. He earned his B.A. from Wake Forest University and an M.A. (Government) from the College of William & Mary. He holds the CPCU designation and specialty designations from the Insurance Institute of America in Risk Management (ARM), Claims (AIC), Management (AIM), and Reinsurance (ARe). He has authored over 500 published articles and ten books on insurance and risk management topics.

Kevin teaches classes in insurance, claims, and risk management for the Washington, D.C., CPCU Chapter, for whom he is a past president. In 1998, he was named "The Standard Setter" by the national CPCU Society for his professional accomplishments and community involvement.

A frequent speaker, trainer, and presenter on topics related to insurance, claims handling, and litigation, he can be reached at kquinley@cox.net (phone 703-652-1320; fax 703-652-1389.) If you are interested in Kevin speaking to your group, please contact him or visit his website at www.kevinquinley.com

Also by Kevin Quinley . . .

Time Management for Claim Professionals

Claims Management

The Quality Plan: Strategies for Keeping Claim Clients Happy

Winning Strategies for Negotiating Claims

Litigation Management

INS 23—Commercial Insurance Course Leaders' Handbook

Managing Product Liability Risk and Avoiding Litigation

Dodging the Bullet: Risk Management Tactics for Physicians that Work

Well-Adjusted: 185 Tips for Adjusters' Career Success

Business at Risk: How to Assess, Mitigate and Respond to Terrorist Threats (with Donald L. Schmidt)

Contributing Author to . . .

Industrial Low Back Pain

The Claims Environment

Principles of Workers Compensation Claims

INS 21—Principles of Insurance Course Leaders' Handbook

INS 22—Personal Insurance Course Leaders' Handbook

CPCU 4—Commercial Liability Risk Management and Insurance Course Leaders' Handbook

Workers Compensation Claims

Acknowledgments

I wish to acknowledge the advice and counsel of the following insurance, claims, and legal professionals who provided invaluable insights. Any errors and omissions are mine, not theirs. Many of these individuals are regular contributors on the Internet risk management discussion forum, RiskMail, which provides a virtual electronic community for ongoing risk management dialogue. I am grateful and indebted to (in no particular order, other than alphabetic):

Richard Ackroyd; Karen Ali; Allan Ballow; Regina Berens; Phil Bly; Thomas Bower, Esq.; David Broussard; Ken Brownlee, CPCU; Charles Chaffin; Nancy Germond;

Bruce Higgins; Jack Jensen; Dave Morgan; Tom Pickhardt; Eric Sieber, CPCU; Brady Smith; William Strachan; Gene Summerlin; Craig Thumel; Beaumont Vance; Patrick Vuchetich; Lyle Walker; and Brad Webb.

Let me single out three more individuals: Barry Zalma, Esq., of Culver City, California, for his prolific insights. For their guru-like expertise in insurance coverage matters, I am indebted to and thank Don Erickson of Murtaugh Miller Meyer & Nelson (Irvine, California) and Erwin Adler of Richards, Watson & Gershon (Los Angeles).

Special thanks go to the terrific folks at the National Underwriter Company, especially my editor, Diana Reitz.

Though an author writes the book, he or she is backed up by a supportive and tolerant family. I am no exception and express my thanks and love to my patient wife, Jane, and to Hunter and Kevin for tolerating a preoccupied spouse and father as he spent time writing another book. May they never need any kind of worst-case survival guide in any realm.

—*Kevin M. Quinley*

Contents

Introduction

"Stuff Happens" to paraphrase a popular bumper sticker.

As claims people, we can all relate to this sentiment. Further, we know what kind of *stuff* the bumper sticker is referencing. Claims people deal with adverse events: fire, theft, accident, injury, hurricane, windstorm, and explosion. Some bad things are acts of nature. Some are manmade.

Some are *micro* and claim-file specific. You are dealing with a difficult claimant, policyholder, claimant attorney, defense attorney, or client. These kinds of claim-file specific problems are too numerous to catalog here. Maybe you get accused of acting in bad faith on a claim. Perhaps your insured tries to threaten you into throwing in your policy limits on a case that you believe is highly defensible. These are examples of claim-file specific challenges.

Other claim headaches are *macro* or operational. They do not necessarily flow from any single claim file. They can, however act as a huge distraction to your—and the staff's—ability to focus on claim handling.

Some bad things befall claim professionals and claim operations. These can throw a claims department into a crisis mode. It can cause panic and despair within the claims professional. The focus of this book is to look at recurring and periodic crises that befall claim professionals and claim operations. Our aim goes beyond identifying these bad things, though. We plan to go a step further and identify ways to deal with, ways to address, and ways to cope with these recurring challenges.

We are not looking to fix blame for the situations. In many cases, these problems arise due to no fault of the claims professional. In some cases, there are issues of poor judgment or inattention. The challenge is to not fix blame but to fix the problem.

In recent years, there has grown an increasing interest in survival. Witness the popularity of TV shows such as *Survivor,* where contestants are exiled to some remote and primitive location and forced to live by their wits. (Perhaps *Survivor* producer Mark Burnette should consider a claims version of the show, giving each contestant a hefty caseload and leaving it to them to organize their own Claims Department!)

Another very popular book is titled, *The Worst Case Scenario Survival Guide.* This instructs readers on how to deal with a daunting array of life-threatening emergencies: airplane crash, drowning, escaping a burning building, bear attacks, etc.

Claim adjusters travel by airplane and occasionally by boat. Unless they are adjusting claims in the backcountry of the Yukon or Tetons, though, they likely won't encounter any Grizzly bears. Nevertheless, adjusters do face an array of daily challenges that can pose worst-case scenarios. These include:

- Getting hit with a bad faith jury award

- Facing a runaway jury verdict

- Being tagged or fined for some market conduct violation

- Suffering a brain drain exodus of the best adjusters

- Making a mistaken hiring decision

- Suffering a natural disaster without having the claims office prepared

- Delivering bad news to bosses

In this book, I have tried to identify major crises that periodically plague claim operations. It does not pretend to be an exhaustive list. Chances are that you can think of other fire drills, crises, and problems. In the interest of brevity, however, I concentrate on a cluster of situations that represent periodic challenges to the productivity, profitability, and smooth running of an effective claims operation.

These crises—in no particular order—are:

- default judgments

- bad faith claims

- a runaway jury award

- having to deliver bad news to the boss

- getting fired or laid off

- having your best claims person quit

- having your recent claims hire turn out to be a dud

- experiencing an insured/policyholder who is non-cooperative or demands that you settle a claim he previously urged you to defend

- being saddled with the psycho-client from hell

- having your defense attorney turn out to be a lemon

- undergoing an audit and/or market conduct examination

- being faced with an influx of new claims from a new account that you're not equipped to service

- experiencing a natural (or man-made) disaster and having to resume operations

There are many other things that add spice and fun to the adjuster's daily job. In winnowing candidate topics, some made the cut and others did not.

This book focuses not so much on the theoretical but the practical aspects of running a busy claims operation. The book is designed for practical use by

- claim adjusters, examiners, supervisors, and managers

- insurance consultants

- in-house claim specialists

- risk managers

- in-house attorneys and legal counsel

Responding to a crisis is an important skill. Perhaps more vital, though, is the ability to prevent crises in the first place. As a result, each chapter includes preventive pointers and tips, ways that companies and adjusters can avoid these problems. The first priority is to put one's finger in the dike. That is the immediate challenge posed by these scenarios. The broader challenge is to step back, figure out what happened, and take steps to ensure that the crisis does not ever happen again. As a wise man once said, "A crisis planned for is no crisis."

I have often said that the best-run claim departments are boring places because they are never in the midst of crises and high drama. If you find you or your claim operation doing periodic fire drills, see it as a red flag danger sign that something is awry. In a boring claim operation, there are few crises or fire drills and no screaming, yelling, or personnel turnover. Given a choice, I'll take boring any day with a claims department that runs like a well-oiled machine. Leave drama to the folks in the theater!

Easy to say—admittedly hard to do. Despite best laid plans, though, we can safely say that as long as there are claim adjusters and claims to handle, there will be crises and worst case scenario situations that erupt. Use this book as a toolbox to prepare yourself—and your department, division, and company—for coping skills when the bad stuff hits the fan.

May you survive and emerge stronger due to the process!

CHAPTER 1

Uh-Oh . . . You're in Default!!

Your insured receives the papers

Your policyholder calls on the phone. He isn't calling to say "Hi" or to shoot the breeze. He isn't phoning to express appreciation for the great job you're doing handling his claims. No—the news is most unnerving.

He says he's holding some legal-looking piece of paper and asks, "What's a default judgment?" These last two words rarely portend good things. You gulp hard. All of a sudden, you don't have an appetite for the chicken salad sandwich you bought for lunch. It doesn't help that it pertains to a claim one of your adjusters is handling and the complaint prays for $1 million. (You're now praying that you can get out of this mess.) The baffled insured promises to fax or send you the motion for default judgment right away.

To rephrase the old introductory line from the Wide World of Sports TV show, you've felt the thrill of victory and now you feel the agony of . . . default.

What will you do?

Work in the field of insurance claims—especially liability claims— long enough and you may encounter the excitement of default judgments. This is one kind of excitement you are better off without, though.

Every adjuster and claims professional should know the meaning of the phrase, default judgment, and its significance. If a defendant in a lawsuit fails to respond to a complaint in the time set by law (often twenty or thirty days), the plaintiff (suer) may request that the default (failure) be entered into the court record by the clerk, which gives the plaintiff the right to a default judgment. The clock starts running when the defendant is served with suit papers. The service may be in person or, perhaps, in some areas, by registered mail.

If the complaint seeks a specific sum of money, the clerk of the court may enter a default judgment. If proof of damages or other relief is necessary, a hearing will follow in which the judge determines terms of the default judgment. In either case, the defendant may not speak on his own behalf. A defendant who fails to file an answer or other legal response when it is due may request that the default be set aside, but when doing so must show a legitimate excuse and a good defense to the lawsuit.

What do you do?

First, find out if a court has actually granted a default. Many times, adjusters say, "We're in default" when, technically, all they mean is that an answer was not timely filed. There is a difference—sometimes a big difference—between seeking a default judgment and actually getting one. Semantics and word choice are important here, but adjusters in a tizzy over defaults can be excused for some imprecision amidst all the excitement. Courts are reluctant to grant default judgments, though one should not base any actions on the optimistic assumption that "everything will be all right."

It's as though you are an emergency room doctor. You must move with that sense of urgency and purpose. Get the patient—i.e., your claim situation—stabilized. As my first boss said when commenting on the adjuster's operational tempo, "Remember—you're driving an ambulance, not a hearse!" So, move with the speed of an ambulance – not a funeral cortege. Here are some tips and suggestions for defusing default judgment time bombs.

Assign to Defense Counsel

Get on the phone posthaste with your friendly local defense attorney. Explain the situation. If your preferred lawyer is out of the office, find out when she will return. If it's not soon—due to trial, vacation or other commitments—ask for a backup lawyer. Fax the suit papers and give the defense attorney enough information to get out of the starting blocks quickly. This is no time to dawdle.

Your marching orders to counsel should be to take immediate action to get the default judgment set aside or vacated. Maybe counsel can file a motion to vacate or set aside the default. Perhaps he can cajole plaintiff's counsel into voluntarily setting it aside. This is where the defense counsel's personal and people skills enter in.

You likely will need to work closely with your attorney. In many cases, you may need to furnish an affidavit explaining what happened. In some areas, excusable neglect or error may be a basis for vacating a default judgment. This is not a nice position to be in, but do whatever you can legitimately to get the default set aside.

Seek a Voluntary Set-aside

Make a direct plea to opposing counsel. In some cases, the adjuster may be able to persuade plaintiff's counsel to voluntarily set aside the default or withdraw the motion for default. In other cases, the opposing counsel may laugh or brush off the adjuster. Still, it never hurts to ask. Perhaps this is an attorney you deal with periodically. If she cuts you a break, there may be an (legitimate) opportunity down the road to do her a favor.

If there is an ongoing relationship—or the prospect of one—there may be a better chance of getting the opposing attorney to voluntarily vacate the default. On the other hand, if you have never dealt with this attorney before and do not expect to do so again, the odds may be slim that opposing counsel will be accommodating.

If you never ask, you'll never know. After all, if the attorney voluntarily withdraws the default, you may not need to go to the expense of engaging defense counsel, or counsel's involvement may be so short-lived that the legal fees will be modest. Swallow your pride and ask. Don't grovel or plead, but at least ask..

What Is the Reason for Default?

Who dropped the ball? Did the suit papers fall through the cracks at the claims office? Did an adjuster file them away without appreciating or realizing their importance? Were suit papers mistaken for another type of document? Did they accidentally get stapled to some other material on another file and get buried there, undetected? Determine how the suit papers came in and the deadline passed without an answer.

If your own defense attorney failed to file an answer in time, there is an opportunity to get acquainted with her errors and omissions (E&O) insurance carrier. It is precisely for these types of attorney glitches that lawyers and law firms buy professional liability insurance coverage. You never want to be in default but, if you are, better that it be someone else's problem and not yours!

On the other hand, did the insured policyholder fail to report the suit papers to you on time? Maybe the person in charge of this was away. Perhaps the papers got lost in the shuffle at the insured's location. Maybe the insured felt that it could do nothing and the matter would go away. Perhaps in the crush of other business and commitments, sheer forgetfulness was the culprit.

Many reasons exist as to why an insured might slip up in reporting suit papers to the insurance company. Whether these are excusable is another issue. If the insured was responsible, it is marginally better for the adjuster. There may be coverage defenses that the insurer can assert if it is not successful in getting the default vacated.

Six Questions to Ask Your Insured

When an insured calls to tell you about receiving a lawsuit, six questions to ask are:

1. On what date were you served?
2. Who received the service of process?
3. How were the suit papers served?
4. Was it a surprise—was there any forewarning?
5. In what state or jurisdiction is the case?
6. How fast can you get the suit papers to me?

Assess whether any coverage issues exist due to the default. That is, did the insured fail to give you timely (or immediate) notice of a lawsuit? Most insurance policies have a strict CONDITIONS section that sets forth clear standards for reporting lawsuits. A common requirement reads as follows:

Condition 2.c. You and any other involved insured must:

(1) Immediately send us copies of any demands, notices, summonses or legal papers received in connection with the claim or a suit.

If the case is in default due to an insured's lapse, consider going immediately into a reservation of rights mode. Basically, you are saying to the insured:

We are going to try to straighten this out. If we do not succeed, however, you may have to absorb this as an uninsured loss due to your breach of a key policy provision.

If you successfully get the default set aside, then it may be a case of no harm no foul and the issue is moot.

If you do not succeed in getting the default set aside, though, the financial loss lies with the policyholder since his lapse or oversight created the problem.

Determine Judicial Tendencies

Determine the leanings of the local court toward defaults. Your local defense attorney should be able to help you here. Some jurisdictions are reluctant to grant default judgments. Others are more willing. In some areas it may hinge on the leanings of the local judges. Ask your counsel the following questions:

- What are our percentage odds of getting out of the default?

- Are courts in this jurisdiction tolerant toward neglect or oversight?

- Will you need an affidavit from us to buttress our explanation for the late response?

- What can we do to improve our odds of having the default vacated?

Discuss with Your Insured

If the lapse was on the part of the insured, get a handle on the reasons and explain the implications. Get a separate statement from the policyholder covering when the suit papers arrived, what (if anything) was done with them, and to whom they were sent. This helps confirm key facts, particularly crucial if there are coverage issues later involving late notice of a lawsuit.

Notify Your E&O Insurer

Who is your E&O carrier? Do you know? Find out. If there is any whiff that the default was due to some claim department oversight, report the matter to the E&O insurer. Avoid the trap of thinking that reporting it to the E&O carrier is tantamount to an admission of guilt, liability, or culpability. Likewise, do not succumb to the temptation of thinking that it will just go away or that it will not amount to anything.

Consider how you view insureds when they use those same lame excuses for not reporting claims and potential losses. Further, you do not want to create a potential coverage situation under your E&O policy through delayed notice of loss. Don't you have enough to worry about with the default without adding the problem of making a mistake with your E&O coverage?

The best maxim is . . . *When in doubt, report it out.* Simply alert your E&O insurer to a possible (or actual) E&O claim. Be a good example to your policyholder. Unless the boss or home office orders you not to report it, make sure that your E&O insurer is aware of the default judgment if your department's action (or inaction) may be a factor.

Of course, in situations in which the default is clearly caused by the insured not complying with loss reporting policy provisions, there may be a tougher call. Some might say that reporting it to the E&O insurer is either premature or unwarranted. Company policy for your own organization may provide guidance.

Ways to Prevent Default Judgments

Flag All Suit Papers

Prominently label or mark any new suit papers that arrive in the daily mail. Work with the mailroom clerk or whoever opens the mail to implement a way to flag suit papers, such as with big red arrow post-it notes, a rubber stamp that says "Suit Papers Attached," or a rule that suit papers go on the top of the pile of mail, lessening the odds that they will be overlooked. Perhaps the incoming mail clerk should compile a central log of suit papers as they arrive, with the claim supervisor or manager getting a copy of the log at the close of each workday.

Of course, this will require that training and coaching for mailroom personnel. You cannot set a high handling priority to items that you cannot see. Not all suit papers arrive screaming their presence as suit papers. Some come attached behind cover letters or *ACORD* loss report forms.

Confusion also arises occasionally due to inconsistency or inaccuracy on how cover letters from insureds or brokers refer to attachments. Some insureds call lawsuits "claims" or "incidents, even though the attachment is really a lawsuit. Some policyholders and insurance brokers are imprecise when using these terms. In some areas, the papers may be called a summons and complaint; in others, a motion for judgment.

In many claim operations, mail clerks are harried and busy. They also are in positions that often experience high turnover. There is a need to train mail personnel on what to look for and how to look beyond the cover letter in deciding how to prioritize or triage incoming mail. This area of training may go beyond what you envisioned for your claims department, but it may be a worthwhile investment for many reasons. You need to minimize the time that any lawsuit paper lingers in the mailroom or is held up for indexing. You need to get it on as soon as possible to the handling adjuster or screening claim supervisor.

No system is 100 percent foolproof, but you should strive to find a way to herald *DANGER—DANGER* when a new lawsuit arrives. You want them to be treated like radioactive hot potatoes.

Build in Redundancy

Have multiple levels of review for each new lawsuit notification. Redundancy is not only a good risk management tool, but it also is a sound claims management practice to further reduce the odds of a default judgment.

Require High Internal Standards

Set and enforce strict internal standards. You should establish standards for timeliness of handling new lawsuits. For example, some offices require that these be assigned to outside counsel within twenty-four hours of receipt or before the sun sets that day. The higher you set the bar, the less chance you'll someday have to sweat it out over a default judgment.

Use Certified Mail

When assigning suit papers to outside counsel, send certified mail, return receipt requested. Better yet, send multiple ways. Build in redundancy.

Acknowledgment from Defense Counsel

Require that defense attorneys affirmatively acknowledge receipt of suit papers within a very tight number of days. When assigning suit papers, set up a diary reminder for a few days later as a reminder to check that the attorney received the papers. Call the attorney if you have not heard from him by the set date to make sure the information was delivered and is receiving attention.

Conduct a Review

When you face a possible default judgment, the number one priority is to get it set aside. Once you do that, make sure to conduct a post-mortem or after action review. Find out what happened and why. Do you need to do a better job of educating policyholders about reporting responsibilities? Do you need to tweak procedures in-house for handling suit papers? Do you have a staff member who fell asleep at the wheel and needs a wake-up call? Much will hinge on who was responsible for causing the problem.

Apply these steps and you will taste the thrill of victory by setting aside the agony of default!

Working with Insurance Brokers to Prevent Defaults

Sometimes default situations occur when suit papers have gone from the insured to a broker, resulting in a delay in reporting the suit to the insurer. This is not a knock on insurance brokers. Many want to be closely involved in the claim-reporting process. They serve a value-added role in playing traffic cop and knowing which new claims go to which insurance carriers.

To be sure, the broker represents the insurance buyer, not the insurance seller. If a lawsuit goes into default because of the intermediary, the insurer may want ask the broker to put its E&O insurer on notice. It is possible that the broker's professional liability insurer will have to answer for the lapse that caused the policy condition to be breached. Clearly, you want to investigate this meticulously before casting any allegations in the broker's direction.

Preventing These Kinds of Problems

Encourage insureds to report claims and lawsuits simultaneously to the insurer and to the broker. This way, the broker stays in the loop, but you avoid bottlenecks that can otherwise occur in new loss reporting.

CHAPTER 2

"Hi, I'm the Sheriff—I Have Some Papers for You."

You and your company are sued for bad faith

Whenever the sheriff arrives, you know the news is not good. He has some papers for you. Now you know what it's like to be a policyholder involved in a claim. Now you get to be the defendant. Not much fun, is it? No sir! The lawsuit names you and your company. It alleges that you have handled a claim poorly and have acted in bad faith. It seeks compensatory and punitive damages. Your head throbs as you start to think of all the things you could have done differently on the case, all the hassle that dealing with this will entail. You're not so detached when you're the defendant in a lawsuit, is it?

Now what will you do?

Being sued for bad faith is never a welcome event, whether you work for an insurance company, an independent adjusting firm, or a third-party claim administrator (TPA). To an extent, it is a fact of life and a cost of doing business. Being sued frequently (and no one can identify the magic numerical threshold) may be a red flag of deeper problems within the claims operation.

On the other hand, let's be realistic. Getting sued for bad faith is a question of *when* rather than *if*. It is somewhat inherent in the nature of the business if you work for an insurer or adjust claims in any line of loss. Don't wear it as a badge of pride. Do not shrug it off as not a big deal. Put it in perspective, though. People sue insurance companies, sometimes without foundation and despite the best efforts to reach an agreement.

When life hands you a bad faith lemon, try to make lemonade. In a way, this may be a good experience, to leaven and broaden your perspective as a claims professional. It's easy for claims people to get jaded and hard bitten, but now you can understand what it feels like to be an insured.

An insured gets sued and fumes indignantly at the claims-handler for having to deal with a frivolous lawsuit. The adjuster has seen it all before—hundreds of times. No big deal. Happens every day. Lawsuits come and lawsuits go. It seems weird if not a little naïve for someone to get distressed over being sued. That's why they buy insurance, isn't it?

Now, though, the shoe (or suit) is on the other foot. You may feel strongly that you or your adjuster did nothing wrong, but you were sued anyway. Now you are the indignant one, spewing on about the unfairness of it all.

Welcome to the world of your policyholder!

Let's take a deep breath and look at a framework for dealing with the bad faith suit.

Review the Complaint

Start as you would (hopefully) on any other kind of suit paper. Carve out some uninterrupted time, take a deep breath, and carefully read the complaint. Center yourself and calm your emotions, which may be churning at this stage. Determine the basis for the complaint. Does it pertain to failure to investigate? Does it involve a first-party claim from your policyholder? Is it a third-party claim from a claimant? Is it rooted in an alleged violation of an Unfair Claim Practice statute? Find out.

Where is the claim file? Is it an open or a closed file? Get a complete copy of it. Who handled the case? Is it an adjuster who is still on staff or one who has left? If the adjuster has left, do you know how to track him down? Do you have a forwarding address? Check with your Human Resources Department to see if the personnel file is available. This department may have information such as the employee's last known address, phone number, and name of emergency contact. Use this information to contact the former employee and get some perspective on how the claim file was handled. Work closely with your Human Resources or Personnel Department to corral this kind of information.

Did they leave voluntarily or were they terminated? Was the departure related to the claim file in question? Did the employee leave on good terms or might he have an axe to grind? These are initial questions that help get the lay of the land regarding any bad faith claim. Answering these questions will help you get organized. It also will assist in determining whether you can expect cooperation or hostility when approaching the ex-employee.

Report the Loss ASAP to Your E&O Insurer

Find out whether your company has errors and omissions (E&O) insurance coverage—hopefully so. Determine the proper procedure for reporting E&O claims and get the claim to the E&O insurer immediately.

It is likely that the E&O policy requires prompt, if not immediate, notice of a new suit.

You may have to dig to learn the identity of the E&O insurer because (hopefully) the odds are that you do not deal with these folks regularly. (If you are dealing with your E&O insurer on a first name basis, that is likely not a good sign!) Find out how the E&O carrier wants to handle assignment of defense counsel. Some have a panel of attorneys from which to choose. Many of these specialize in handling insurance bad faith cases.

In other instances, the E&O insurer may let you select counsel of your choice and direct that counsel to report to the E&O carrier. The answer may hinge on whether you have a first-dollar E&O policy or some sort of deductible or self-insured retention. You may or may not feel comfortable picking the defense attorney. The lawyers you deal with regularly may not have expertise in insurance bad faith defense.

In any event, meet with defense counsel. Send the complaint to the selected defense attorney as soon as possible so that the court docket is protected and there is no chance of a default judgment.

Often, the E&O carrier will want a complete copy of the claim file. If so, ship it to the E&O carrier.

Also inquire about reporting flow. Ask to be copied in on all reports and correspondence from the defense attorney handling the bad faith claim. How often does the E&O insurer want reports? To whom should they go?

Be careful what you put in writing after the bad faith claim has been made. Once the file is in suit, make sure that any communication you initiate and anything you write is protected by attorney-client privilege. Write everything as though it will ultimately be discoverable—even if it isn't. The last thing you want or need is an email to your boss or the Home Office on the order of:

"Adjuster Bob just made another mistake that has gotten us sued for bad faith"

Or

"I knew something like this was bound to happen sooner or later."

Or

"Now you know why we fired her."

The attorney pursuing the bad faith claim can have a field day with such comments. Do not naively think that just because your note, communiqué, or email is not part of the claim file it's not discoverable.

Electronic discovery is an increasingly popular area for inquiry by enterprising claimant attorneys. Old emails may be retrievable from hard drives, backup tapes, or other archived media. **Moral:** Watch what you say.

> ### Recap of Questions to Ask and Answer
>
> - Is this an open or closed claim file?
> - Has the case been settled or not?
> - Does the claim file reflect that this situation was brewing?
> - If the file is still open, should it be kept with the current adjuster or reassigned?
> - Are there any legal or defensibility implications with reassigning the case to a different adjuster?
> - If the adjuster whose actions are under question is a former employee, do you know how to reach him? Did he leave on good terms?
> - Are there any regulatory implications? Has any complaint been lodged with the state insurance department?
> - Is the plaintiff a current policyholder or an ex-insured?
> - Is there still an ongoing business relationship?
> - Exactly what is the nature of the alleged bad faith?

Check Out the Plaintiff Attorney

Ever heard of her before? What is her specialty? What is the caliber of the opposition? Check it out. Look up the attorney's background in resources such as Martindale Hubbell (http://lawyers.martindale.com/xp/Martindale/home.xml).

In addition, put the attorney's name in an Internet search engine (such as www.google.com) and see what surfaces.

Do not phone the opposing attorney to discuss the case or to explore settlement unless you have approval to do this from your E&O insurer.

Provide a Heads-up

Alert your boss and Home Office personnel if you think a lawsuit may be coming. Dust off and consult your procedure manual to see what it says about handling lawsuits against the company.

Be Sensitive about the Perils of Electronic Communication

Email has the illusion of privacy. That's all that it is, an illusion. Unfortunately, people let their hair down in email in a way that they would not in a fax, letter, or hard copy memo. Off the cuff, facetious, or flip statements in an email can come back to haunt the adjuster (and claim operation).

Don't think that hitting the "Delete" key is a solution, either. In the computer realm, deleted does not mean gone forever. Often there are ways to retrieve past emails through tape backups or some archive system employed by businesses as part of their Information Technology disaster recovery program.

Plaintiff attorneys are not dumb. They know this. In an increasing amount of litigation, discovery includes a request for production for copies of past emails. (Courts do not care much about how expensive it is to retrieve them or how many man-hours it will take.) During the Department of Justice antitrust trial against Microsoft, some of the government's best evidence was copies of emails from Bill Gates to others, talking about how to take advantage of competitors.

Unfortunately, email may produce golden nuggets for the plaintiff in bad faith suits. Do not give them any new opportunities to pan for gold in your stream! Consider adjuster emails produced to a jury along the following lines:

"This insured is a jerk and the claim should be resisted."

"We owe the claim but are under orders from corporate to reduce loss payouts."

"We owe the claim but should slow down claim payments to help out cash flow."

"The insured seems to be a professional claimant."

"This claimant attorney is a real pain—let him sweat it out."

"If we pay or cover this loss, there's no way we'll meet our financial targets."

"If we pay this claim, our bonus for the year is gone."

"Can we delay payment a bit while we squeeze more yield out of our investments?"

Turn a Negative into a Positive

There is a school of thought that by fixating on bad faith, bad faith, bad faith it may become a self-fulfilling prophecy. It's like telling yourself while hitting a golf drive, "Don't lift your head!" or, during a tennis stroke, "Don't bend your elbow!" Your mind hears, "Lift your head" and "Bend your elbow" and you may do just that.

Better to have a self-talk that says, "Keep the head down!" or "Arm straight!" Better to focus on a positive than a negative. What implications does this have for bad faith loss prevention? Plenty!

Rather than obsess about avoiding the landmines of bad faith, think of how you can promote good faith claim-handling practices within your shop. Accentuate the positive. How can you demonstrate good faith? (There has even been an Insurance Institute of American textbook for the Associate in Claims (AIC) program entitled, *Aggressive Good Faith*, which sounds like an oxymoron if there ever was one!) This is more than a mere semantic point.

Seek Outside Help

Periodically invite an insurance coverage attorney in to talk with your staff about good faith and bad faith. Pick one with expertise in defending insurance companies. Many of them have the scar tissue from prior experience to understand the soft spots and vulnerabilities that can plague a claims operation. They see what works and what doesn't in bad faith defense. Many of these attorneys are willing (if not happy) to conduct informal service training with your staff, often pro bono and off the meter. Your staff members benefit because they learn ways to stay out of trouble. The attorney benefits by developing good karma and relationships that may enhance business development. When time comes to assign a coverage matter, whom do you suppose the adjusters will call? Attorneys making these presentations cultivate good top-of-mind awareness from adjusters who may later refer cases to them.

Be creative in organizing such forums. Once I was at a claims conference and heard a dynamite presentation on "The Ten Commandments of Bad Faith" by a Los Angeles-based coverage attorney. I was very impressed and keen on my claim staff hearing it too. Small problem: my office is located nearly 3,000 miles from Los Angeles, in a suburb of Washington, D.C. I approached the attorney later at the conference and proposed that he give his seventy-five-minute presentation by speakerphone, from his office in Los Angeles to a conference room in Chantilly, Virginia. It saved the attorney tons of travel time and air fare expense yet delivered a very effective message on bad faith prevention, complete with handouts and post-presentation question and answer session. We did not rent some expensive teleconference facility, though even that may have been cheaper than flying the attorney from coast to coast. **Moral:** Explore creative options to see how you can deliver periodic good faith training to your claims staff.

Urge the Claim Staff to Embrace the New York Times *Standard*

Have each ask, "Would I mind seeing this email published on the front page of the *New York Times*?" before clicking the "send" button.

The flip side is that emails can show good faith if the electronic paper trail evidences that the adjuster was bending over backwards to be fair, to give policyholders the benefit of the doubt, and to speed the claim to conclusion.

Establish Specific Good Faith Claim Standards

Do this within your department and periodically audit files for compliance. These should revolve around the areas of

- prompt investigation standards

- clear recitation and/or explanation of policy provisions

- quick acknowledgement of and answers to any communication from insureds

- use of outside coverage counsel as a guide or sounding board in gray area cases, complex situations, or where the stakes are high

Barry Zalma, an insurance coverage attorney from Culver City, California, states,

I would not be concerned at all [about being sued for bad faith] since, first, I cannot—as an employee of an insurance company— breach the covenant of good faith and fair dealing since I am not a party to the contract. The case should be immediately dismissed as to me. See *Gruenberg v. Aetna*, 108 Cal. Rptr. 480 (1973).

Further, since I was acting for my employer, as an agent of a disclosed principal I am not liable to the plaintiff, and my employer is obligated to defend and indemnify me.

My head doesn't throb since I am in California and this happens all the time. I have contacted my personal lawyer—if I have one— and if not one of the defense counsel we use to start preparing my counterattack.

First, I demand dismissal or else. If not, I get the case dismissed and then I sue the lawyer and the plaintiff for malicious prosecution. I retire on the proceeds.

Until recently, I and just about every claims person in California were sued for bad faith when claims were denied to allow the plaintiff to destroy diversity and avoid federal court where the law was somewhat more favorable to insurers. It got annoying and expensive and did not stop until I filed multiple malicious prosecution actions after defeating the spurious claim.

It is surprising that this tort that, unfortunately, was born in the fair state of California has been adopted by most states but is applied differently in almost every one of them. Here in California, the party must be a party to the contract in order to be effectively sued for bad faith.

Of course, no matter how egregious the conduct of insureds, they cannot be sued for the tort in California. What is sauce for the goose is not sauce for the gander.

Ken Brownlee of Atlanta, Georgia, former corporate risk manager for an international TPA states,

A bad faith allegation need not be bad news UNLESS one has been a bad boy! Most bad faith claims don't come as a shock to the insurer. The majority results from cases of failure to pay policy limits where the insurer should have done so, with a resulting excess verdict from the jury. The insurer will—or ought to—know about this long before the insured is forced to file a lawsuit. If it doesn't, it's asleep at the switch. (But then it probably was asleep at the switch for failing to pay policy limits if appropriate in the first place.)

If it wasn't a policy limits case, then likely the insurer will appeal the excess verdict on behalf of its insured and try to turn the situation around.

There are, of course, bad faith cases that derive from being a bad boy, and those, I suppose, do come as a shock to those involved. But here again, it's a matter of good litigation management. A bad faith suit is little different from any suit seeking punitive damages. First, the laws differ by state and need to be researched. Then one practices *Sermon of the Mount* risk management: Make peace with your accuser while you are on the way to the courthouse.

Once the bad faith claim is concluded, there may be some vital loose ends to tie up. As traumatic and distressing as the experience is, try to learn from it. Postmortem the claim file to see what you could have done differently to prevent a bad faith claim. Would doing things differently have created other problems?

After battle drills, the U.S. Army conducts a discipline called *after action reviews*. After patient deaths, teaching hospitals conduct M&M sessions—morbidity and mortality conferences. The aim in both is not to affix blame, but to fix a problem. Apply this discipline to learn from nettlesome claim situations and to prevent future bad faith claims.

Ten Commandments for Minimizing Potential Bad Faith Lawsuits

By Erwin E. Adler

Erwin E. Adler is director of the insurance department for the Los Angeles, San Francisco, and Orange County offices of Richards, Watson & Gershon (http://www.rwglaw.com/). He developed the following to assist claim professionals avoid or minimize bad faith lawsuits. His complete presentation on the subject was made at the 2002 ACE/SCLA National Conference.

Mr. Adler's presentation centers on the idea that the claim file tells the story of the claim. In summarizing his analysis, Mr. Adler states that the adjuster's basic goal is simple: the claims professional desires to show that he or she is doing a good job in a demanding environment and has thoroughly documented the effort to thoroughly investigate and to promptly pay the claim. He refers to the claim file as a letter that is being written for a jury:

The Ten Commandments

At bottom, the claims professional, <u>not</u> the policyholder's counsel, is the author of the letter that the jury will receive. Further, the following commandments governing "letter-writing" are predicated upon the Golden Rule for claims professionals, viz., before the adjuster places any comment in the claims file, the comment must pass the following basic test:

Is the comment or statement necessary so that I can make a business decision or otherwise evaluate this claim on the merits?

In short, will the letter be a "love letter" or a "poison pen letter"? Only the claims professional has the ability to write that letter, and he or she should consider the following guidelines in writing that "letter":

I. Thou Shalt Make a Complete Record of the Claims Handling Process in the Log Notes (or Equivalent System)

Since the claims professional controls the claims file, he or she can set forth a full record of the case, *viz,* explain the diligent efforts which went into investigating the underlying claims and the related coverage issues. Be diligent in recording conversations, documenting the investigation, and following up the outstanding issues. These efforts will maximize the probability that the jury will perceive that the carrier has acted in good faith.

II. Thou Shalt Answer Every Question Raised in the Claims File

Assuming that a claim raises questions (as most significant claims do), the claims professional must answer them. At a minimum, unanswered questions in a claims file raise an inference in the mind of the jury that the carrier did not adequately or completely investigate the claim. At worst, they raise the inference of a conspiracy by the carrier to deprive a policyholder of policy benefits.

III. Any Referral of a Coverage (or Other) Questions to Counsel Shall Be a Benefit, Not a Burden, to the Policyholder

Coverage questions need to be answered. The claims professional, however, cannot forget he or she is in control of and responsible for writing a "love letter" to the jury. Thus, in referring such a question to counsel, increase the probability of the jury perceiving this referral to be a benefit to the policyholder by providing the policyholder with a "second chance" for coverage rather than creating an inference that the adjuster conspired with counsel to deprive the policyholder of coverage.

IV. Thou Shalt Not Refer or Consider the Financial Condition of the Policyholder or Third-Party Claimant Before Deciding Whether to Pay the Claim

No business purpose is served by considering the financial condition of the policyholder or the third party claimant. At bottom, whether the claim involves a pauper or a plutocrat, the claim professional cannot consider the person's financial condition in deciding whether to pay a claim.

V.   Thou Shalt Not Refer to the Race, Religion, Gender, or Ethnic Background of the Claimant or Third Party

Again these issues are totally irrelevant to deciding whether to cover a claim. Moreover, it is generally illegal for a claims professional to consider race, religion, gender, or ethnic background before deciding whether to pay a claim. A jury could easily perceive such unnecessary comments as demonstrating that the carrier deprived someone of their rights for an improper motive. Put another way, the policyholder's counsel will argue that such comments disclose why the carrier "abandoned the insured in his time of need."

VI. Thou Shalt Not Use Humor in a Claims File

The butt of humor by the claims person will inevitably be the claimant or the policyholder. Since the jury is comprised of a group of policyholders, it is more likely to identify itself with the butt of that humor—the policyholder or the claimant—rather than the claims professional. Such comments do not create any positive benefit for the carrier.

VII. Thou Shalt Not Report Unsubstantiated Rumors

On the one hand, claims must be resolved upon the facts. On the other, claims cannot be resolved on the basis of vague rumors or unsubstantiated theories. Reliance on rumors tends to support the policyholder's theory that the carrier indulged in such speculation to avoid paying a lawfully due claim.

VIII.The Claims File Should Not Include Any Criticism of the Line Adjuster

Recognizing that the claims file will probably be read by a jury, there is no place for criticism of fellow claims people. Such managerial criticism directly highlights the incompetence of those handling the claim and indirectly raises the inference that the carrier improperly denied the claim.

IX. Thou Shalt Not Evaluate the Judge Unless You Personally Know the Judge; If You Rely on the Advice of Counsel, Say So

Plainly, evaluating the judge may be important. If, however, you obtain the evaluation of counsel, so note the claims file rather than stating counsel's opinion to be your own.

X. *Thou Shalt Not Evaluate Opposing Counsel Unless Personally Knowledgeable Enough about that Counsel to Do So*

Unless you are knowledgeable about and capable of independently evaluating opposing counsel, rewriting your counsel's evaluation of their adversary will not be ultimately helpful to you or your carrier.

CHAPTER 3

Sock It to Me...

The jury returns with a runaway award

Now you know why comedian Whoopi Goldberg said, "I wouldn't want to trust my fate to twelve people who were too dumb to get out of jury duty."

The jury has spoken and the news is not good. You thought you would win the trial. In the alternative, you thought that an adverse award would be well within your reserve and your assessment. In fact, your defense attorney agreed.

The jury saw things differently, though. They returned a multi-million-dollar award. Remember when million dollar awards were notable? Those times now seem so quaint. Million dollar awards are routine these days. We've become anesthetized. Heck, now there are Carl Sagan-esque awards—"billions and billions." Perhaps the jury added a punitive damage award—just for good measure. (You're not so sure that your policy covers that, by the way.) Maybe the entire award was for compensatory damages—not punitive—but the award exceeds your insurance policy limit. Maybe your good insured has excess coverage, maybe not. In either event, you are in for some very exciting times.

What will you do now?

According to *Punitive Damages: How Juries Decide*, a book by a group of economists and legal scholars (Cass Sunstein Ed., et al, University of Chicago Press: 2002), juries are quick to impose harsh penalties. Using mock trials, the authors found that jurors systematically ignore judges' instructions, are easily swayed by amounts requested by plaintiffs, and mete out overly harsh punishments to companies for failing to deal with low-probability risks that they themselves wouldn't have addressed had they been running the companies.

Six Questions to Ask Defense Counsel during Trial

During trial, always keep one eye on breaking developments and another eye on the prospect of an appeal should things turn sour. Each day, ask your defense counsel the following questions:

1. What happened today—very briefly and in summary form?

2. Were there any surprises? Any development that caught us unawares?

3. On balance, was today good, bad, or indifferent for our case?

4. What happens tomorrow?

5. Based on everything that has happened thus far, is there any material change in your valuation of this case?

6. Has anything happened in the trial thus far than could preserve our right of appeal if the case goes bad?

If the jury rocks your world with a jumbo or unexpected verdict, encourage your counsel to preserve the record for a possible appeal. Preserving the record might include admitting (over objection) so-called expert testimony that fails the sniff test. It might be admission of evidence that is irrelevant, prejudicial, or should be inadmissible. It might be erroneous charges that the judge gave to the jury. Defense counsel should preserve any and all bases for appeal in order to step back and reassess options if, despite the best of efforts, the jury delivers a runaway award.

Filing an Appeal

Instruct your defense attorney to immediately file an appeal. There may even be some other steps that defense counsel can take, such as moving for a judgment notwithstanding verdict (J.N.O.V.). The immediate aim is to do anything to get the award set aside and to signal to the other side your intention of fighting the matter. This very act may impart some flexibility to the other side.

Judgment notwithstanding the verdict, or J.N.O.V. for short (Latin: Judgment Non Obstante Veredicto) is the practice in American courts whereby the presiding judge may overrule the jury's decision and reverse or amend its verdict. More often requested in civil cases, this remedy permits the judge to exercise discretion to alter a judgment which cannot stand as a matter of law. A losing attorney's motion for a J.N.O.V. is rarely granted by judges, and only in cases, for example, where a jury awards civil damages that are grossly excessive, grossly inadequate, or wholly unsupportable by law. In criminal cases in the U.S., only the defendant (and not the prosecution) may move for a J.N.O.V.

Remittitur, To send a case back to the lower court from which an appeal was taken.

Generally, in my experience, judges are reluctant to reverse a large verdict or award. It seems to almost never happen. Judges rationalize that the jury has spoken and that, if an error has occurred, an appellate court should make that determination. Still, it never hurts to try. (These are the same judges who tend to let in all evidence and say that the jury can decide how much or how little weight to give it.)

If you appeal a decision or award, the insured may have to post an appeal bond. The adjuster is often not obligated to obtain the bond, but it may fall to the adjuster to walk the insured through the process. The defense attorney may also have some insight on navigating this process. Many insurance policies state that the insurer pays the premium on an appeal bond (often under the Supplementary Payments portion of the policy) but is not obligated to actually provide it.

Getting an appeal on record is one step in buying time within which to assess or reassess strategy. Occasionally, the appealing party must also request and pay for a complete trial transcript. This can also be a laborious and expensive process.

Choosing Counsel

Once you note an appeal, there usually follows a briefing and hearing schedule. One issue to ponder is: do you let the attorney and firm that handled the underlying trial handle the appeal as well? This is an important decision that may have implications for the odds of winning or losing. Let's discuss the pros and cons of that decision.

The best law firm for the trial may or may not be the best firm for the appeal. Often you are in this situation because trial counsel was off target in assessing the percentage odds of victory or the size of the award. Let's see— he was off base on the underlying case so now you want to entrust the appeal to him? Also, trial counsel may be too close to the case to be totally objective. Counsel may be too emotionally involved. It may be useful to get a fresh set of eyes and ears on a case to bolster the strength of the appeal or to weigh dispassionately its odds of success.

In addition, different skill sets are at play here. Some firms have a strong appellate practice. Others do not. You may need to probe a bit because some law firms are reluctant to admit that they are not skilled at virtually anything.

Ask trial counsel about the strength of the firm's appellate practice. It is tempting for the sake of convenience to keep the appeal with the same firm that handled the trial. One plus is that they are already familiar with the case.

Moving the case to a different firm for the appeal involves extra time and effort. The appellate firm may need some time (and money) to get up to speed, especially since trial counsel may not be overwhelmingly cooperative if she views the transfer as a vote of no confidence. Diplomacy and tact on the adjuster's part can navigate this, though.

Review Reserves in Light of the Award and Appeal

Further, take another look at the reserves for adequacy in terms of indemnity and expense. Indemnity/claim reserves may need to be hiked in order to align them with the jury award. Also, look at either post or pre-judgment interest. Different companies have different reserve philosophies on such points. Some may want to factor in the percentage odds of a successful appeal. Others may want to reserve to full value of the appeal. Determine and learn your own company's philosophy.

The expense reserve may also need a large boost. One prime reason for this is that the legal meter will run from trial transcripts and appellate costs. This must be factored in to a realistic expense reserve.

Other Actions

Alert the boss. Bad news does travel downhill; make sure in this case that it travels uphill as well. The boss needs to know about a whopping jury award. Do not let the first notice be her reading about it in the newspapers or seeing an astronomical reserve hike in the monthly figures. Tell the boss what happened and what you plan to do about it (appeal, pay the award, negotiate a discounted settlement pending appeal, etc.) Bad news with the boss goes down worse when the boss is surprised.

Antidote: practice damage (and spin) control by getting to the boss promptly, not in a tizzy or a state of panic, but by laying out what happened and what your options are now. Delivering the news won't get any easier if you put it off. Don't you have enough to worry about on the jury award itself without adding some angst over alerting the boss?

Better still to alert—prior to trial—the boss to the trial, its exposure, and the possibility that an adverse result is not out of the question.

Alert the insurance broker. Much of the same rationale about alerting the boss applies here. The insured's broker (or agent) may learn about it sooner or later. Might as well make it sooner. Explain that you fought the good fight, thought you had a good chance to win the case but that—as is often the case—the jury saw things differently. At least you showed that you were willing to go into court and fight for your policyholder. You did not throw in the towel. Nor are you inclined to wave the white flag now. Who knows—you may be able to turn this negative (losing the trial) into a positive (loyalty to policyholders by fighting for them in court).

Alert the excess carrier. Hopefully, you have already put them on notice but, if not, better late than never.

Consult with the insured. Commiserate with the insured's representatives and plot strategy. Do they want to fight the award? Do they want it paid? You are not necessarily bound by their preference here, but it helps to know whether you may be facing a two-front war: one with the plaintiff and one with the insured over strategy.

Alert the reinsurer. Be attuned to any reinsurance implications. Part of the award may be covered by reinsurance. You do not want to violate the reinsurance treaty through any slip-up in loss reporting. Comply and report. Even if you are technically late under the reinsurance treaty because you thought there was no way the award would be sufficiently large to tap reinsurance, better late than never when it comes to reinsurance reporting.

A Defense Attorney's Perspective

Gene Summerlin, of Ogborn Summerlin & Ogborn, Lincoln, Nebraska, states:

> From a lawyer's perspective, and aside from the obvious steps that one would take to protect the insured's legal rights, now is the time to deconstruct why the attorneys' and claim personnel's judgments were off base. Post verdict juror interviews conducted by trained professionals can provide valuable insight into what went wrong. The key is to determine whether this truly was a situation in which the jury went crazy (in which case there

is really not much one can do) or whether the defense misunderstood or missed a key element of the case that allowed an unexpected verdict.

Case in point: A manufacturer had suffered significant losses in defending products suits on one of its industrial tools. The verdicts were fairly consistent and coming from a wide range of geographical regions. The basic defense in these cases had been that the product wasn't dangerous and the injuries were caused by misuse. Juries obviously were not buying it. When the manufacturer began conducting post juror interviews followed up by focus groups, we learned that laypeople were looking at this product as obviously dangerous. The claim that the product wasn't dangerous diluted the force of the misuse theory. When the manufacturer began defending the cases by saying that the product was obviously dangerous—but not UNREASONABLY dangerous (the legal standard)—and the injury was caused by misuse, the manufacturer started getting defense verdicts and much lower awards of damages when a plaintiff's verdict was returned.

Obviously, not every unexpected verdict justifies extensive deconstruction, but I am amazed that many attorneys and clients who are thorough in preparing for trial are lax in analyzing what can be learned post trial—in both wins and losses.

Lyle Walker, President of Walker Risk Management (Allen Park, Michigan) says that asking, "What do you do?" when there's an unexpectedly large award is like asking God, `Why am I dead?' At that point, Walker says, it is a little late to be asking. But, in this case, he gives three bits of advice:

1. Find the resources to fund the unexpected loss.

2. Examine the cause and what preventative measures can be taken to avoid the calamity in the future.

3. Consider hiring another attorney to mount an appeal.

> *Legal Steps to Forestall the Freakish Award*
>
> 1. Go for a judgment N.O.V.;
> 2. A remittitur; or
> 3. Exercise your appellate rights.

Eric Sieber, CPCU, AIC, RPA, of E.J. Sieber & Company in Alta Loma, California, recommends a methodical approach in these scenarios:

Try and determine what went wrong. One good way to gain insight into what happened (along with possibly finding justification for a motion for new trial) is to conduct a postmortem by interviewing the jurors. Whenever an excess verdict occurs, the wheels immediately start in motion for my office to get the necessary info to begin contacting jurors, etc., as we meet with trial counsel and the claim representative. It is interesting to see how few claims executives have a plan in place for when the jury socks it to them.

Engage a Pretrial Focus Group

Let's step back for a moment to a time before the bad stuff hits the fan, before the jury returns with its freakish award. There may be ways to assess whether the way you view reality and case value comports with the way a lay jury would view reality and case value. For example, before trial—especially a high stakes trial—consider engaging a focus group or conducting a mock trial. This may provide a weathervane on the likelihood of getting popped big time.

Of course, some claims people (and lawyers) swear by such techniques. Others swear at them. These avenues are often quite expensive, which is one deterrent. You are already likely incurring massive expenses for trial preparation—attorney time, expert prep, witness preparation, motions, etc. On top of that, you're going to hire what?!

Due to the expense of a focus group, an alternative may be one of the various computerized tools that simulate mock trials or mock jury deliberations. (I often remark tongue in cheek, "Mock juries need not deliver mock justice—enough of that is delivered by real juries!") We should start this discussion with one reason why such computerized tools are alluring to insurance companies and claim operations. Turnover rates are so high within many insurance companies and claims operations that employers struggle to find ways to impart seasoning and insight to evaluating personal injury cases. It is hard to retain experienced claim professionals. Since the good ones are often scarce, they are in demand and are highly mobile in pursuing emerging job opportunities.

Even in claim departments that have seasoned professionals, they are often so busy handling their own caseloads and administrative duties that they lack the time to train and mentor newer adjusters. In a perfect world, an insurer or claims adjusting company would have the seasoned veteran imbue the younger practitioners with the tricks of the trade that enter into claim valuations. Without putting in the same amount of time, the newer adjusters could compress the learning curve by emulating or replicating claim valuation methods used by their counterparts who were seasoned after decades of claim-handling experience.

Claim departments do not function in a perfect world, though. Caseloads are high and often unpredictable. Job mobility is pronounced in claims work, and it is often difficult to retain staff with lengthy tenure. Administrative demands and corporate reorganizations from on high at corporate often consume huge chunks of time. The challenge for insurers is to train newer, less seasoned claims staff and empower them with analytical tools that can enable them to better evaluate cases. This challenge has spawned a mini-industry of computer software tools that aim to render more reliable and scientific the *art* of evaluating the worth of personal injury claims.

Jury Simulation and Valuation Models

Colossus

Another analytical tool available to insurance claim adjusters is a proprietary software system known as *Colossus*, developed by CSC (Computer Sciences Corporation), El Segundo, California. Over forty property and casualty insurance companies license the *Colossus* system as a knowledge-based tool for insurance adjusters to use in evaluating personal injury claims.

One publicized example of using *Colossus* involved Allstate Insurance Company. This major insurer faced allegations that it used the software to greatly reduce claim payouts. Allegedly, one method was to bore in on unrepresented claimants to convince them that the adjuster was representing their interests. Some states held that this ran afoul of unauthorized practice of law.

Another component of this campaign is use of *Colossus* claim evaluation software to price injury claims and to remove elements of adjuster subjectivity from the process. The insurance industry's use of *Colossus* has led to some state trial lawyer associations hosting seminars that explain the *Colossus* system and its impact on negotiating bodily injury claims with insurance adjusters.

Jury Verdict Research®

Another analytical tool is available to claim professionals from Jury Verdict Research, a division of LRP Publications, Horsham, Pennsylvania. Based on the most recent verdicts and settlements in Jury Verdict Research's® 186,000-case database, Case Evaluation Software and the Basic Settlement Module will calculate the probable verdict, settlement amount, and chance of a plaintiff verdict. The proprietary software adjusts for case-specific facts such as injury and liability situation, amount of medical expenses, lost wages, location of trial, effect of permanent impairment and more. In minutes, the vendor says that the user receives a detailed, easy-to-read report to support an offer during mediations or client counseling.

Litigation over Computerized Valuation Tools

Use of software evaluation tools to assess claims has not been without controversy. In 2003, a Redmond, Washington, woman filed a bad faith lawsuit against Farmers Insurance Company of Washington (Farmers) accusing the company of systematically using the computer program called *Colossus* to provide an inaccurately low evaluation of her severe injuries in order to artificially reduce settlement offers.

According to the lawsuit, Farmers used *Colossus* to evaluate Barbara Martin's insurance claims arising from a serious automobile accident. As a result, the complaint alleged, Farmers assigned an intentionally low value to Martin's injuries and refused to pay her claim against her underinsured motorist (UIM) coverage. An arbitrator later determined the value of Martin and her family's damages, which included debilitating back injuries, resulting depression, lost wages, and a diminished ability to interact with her husband, son, and baby daughter, at $377,000.

After the arbitration, Farmers paid the UIM policy limits. This lawsuit seeks additional damages for breach of contract and anti-consumer practices.

The complaint alleges that Farmers based its settlement offers on figures provided by *Colossus*, effectively eliminating the ability of a human adjuster to evaluate a comprehensive view of an insured's case. The program works when an insurance adjuster enters data and categorical information from medical records. *Colossus* then accesses a complex set of rules to decide the value of more than 600 trauma-induced injuries. However, the program doesn't account for intangibles, such as the lost ability to care for a child, the suit states.

The lawsuit states that the nature of the program's data-entry and computation features results in artificially low settlement figures, allowing Farmers to effectively profit from claims rather than provide reasonable compensation to injured claimants. In addition, Farmers exacerbates the profiteering by creating compensation incentives for employees tied to the low settlement figures, according to the complaint.

According to Computer Services Corporation, the maker of *Colossus*, thirteen of the top twenty U.S. Property and Casualty Insurers use the software to evaluate bodily injury claims. However, insurance companies and agents do not disclose the existence of the program, the complaint states.

This is believed to be the first case brought in the United States specifically based on using *Colossus* for claims adjustment.

In April 1999, as Martin slowed for traffic on the I-90 bridge, a large SUV rearended her car, slamming the vehicle across two lanes with such force that it ripped the driver's bucket seat from the vehicle chassis. The accident left Martin with severe injuries to her spine and neck, which caused chronic back pain and debilitating headaches that, according to doctors, will require a lifetime of care.

After the accident, the negligent driver's insurance company paid Martin $100,000, acknowledging that her damages were actually greater than the available coverage. Farmers saw things differently, according to the complaint. Although Martin's UIM policy provided for $100,000 in addition to what the negligent driver covered, Farmers declined to offer anything for damages, based on an artificially low *Colossus* evaluation, the suit alleged.

After nearly three years of trying unsuccessfully to obtain a fair settlement from Farmers, Martin went through arbitration in February 2003. The lawsuit named defendants Farmers Insurance Company of Washington, Farmers Group, Inc., and Farmers Insurance Exchange.

Caveats and Opportunities

Analytical evaluation tools will never and should never substitute for the reasoned and seasoned judgment of the claims professional. Nevertheless, they have many potential benefits as an adjunct to historical/conventional claim valuation techniques.

First, the results may avoid the incurring of a significant investment of time. They let adjusters analyze possible trial success versus anticipated trial and legal expenses. This lets the claim professional decide whether the outlay of time and expense (time/fees to prepare a case for trial and through trial) is economical and the risk acceptable, or whether settlement with the opposing counsel should be revisited. Before you decide to file the suit or go to trial, the results of such analytical tools help justify your expenditure of time and effort. Such tools can also reinforce confidence in your decision-making process. If there are client control issues, the fruits of such tools may help realistically calibrate your policyholder's expectations.

Second, improved results may flow from the increased strength of your negotiating position by having such independent data to support your valuation. It can become a compelling talking point in settlement discussions with attorneys. You may be in a much better position to convince the claimant or the plaintiff attorney to accept your valuation and offer. You can raise serious questions about the attorney's basis for her settlement offers, especially if they fall into the pie in the sky category. This can help extract concessions during the dynamic of settlement negotiations.

Third, an independent valuation might also be used as a hedge in bad faith claims by showing the reasonableness of an insurance adjuster's opinion. Analytical tools may enable practitioners to provide detailed analyses of profile responses, identify trends, or analyze case material.

Further, these tools may also provide a means of support to boost adjuster productivity. Through the Internet, the Settlement Research Group can provide polling services for about 325 cities throughout the United States. Harris Interactive, Inc., facilitates the polling. Harris has been conducting market research for over forty years, producing the well-known Harris Public Opinion Poll.

The arena of computers and information technology has an acronym, GIGO, which may be apropos here. GIGO stands for garbage in—garbage out. Computers can do lots of interesting things, but the quality of their output relates to the quality of the information put into them. Bad data or assumptions going in equals bad conclusions coming out.

One challenge for even the most conscientious adjuster arises from the possibility that the adjuster may rarely (if ever) actually step foot inside a courtroom or see defense counsel in action at trial. Many claim adjusters are so busy pushing paper, moving a monumental caseload of files, and doing administrative busy-work imposed from above that they cannot afford the time or luxury of seeing how claims actually progress through the litigation process.

The notion of taking a week or two to observe a trial is laughable to most claim adjusters. While many (perhaps most) would like to do this, insurance companies cannot make money if their claim adjusters are tied up out of the office on one file for a week or more at a time.

Most adjusters don't like this situation or arrange matters this way. Higher-ups may tolerate high caseload averages per adjuster in order to minimize fixed costs and employee salary overhead. In fairness to insurance adjusters, their caseloads simply can't be compared with those of attorneys. A personal injury attorney may, at any one time, handle, say, forty to fifty cases.

By contrast, it is not unusual for an insurance claims adjuster to handle 200, 300, or even 400 files. Give an attorney this many cases and see how she reacts, how quality-focused she becomes, or how she views the prospect of spending a week or two in the courtroom while work piles up on the other 399 (unattended) files. It might change one's perspective.

As a result, like it or not, some claim adjusters may take their knowledge of the courtroom from watching reruns of *Ally McBeal* or *The Practice*. While these make for entertaining television, what TV-watching does not produce is an authoritative sense of how juries view cases, one key component in claim valuation. It is also a component that no computer or software—regardless of high-tech bells and whistles—can replicate.

Some adjusters find the software used to evaluate claims of dubious value. If clients wanted software to determine the value of a loss, the American judiciary might have opted for computers for juries.

Consider for a moment a gray area case of liability. Damages are substantial, perhaps $200,000. Liability is contested. There may be a 50 percent chance that a jury will find that the defendant liable. That could yield a judgment of zero or a deeply discounted award. If the jury finds that the defendant was liable, though, the award could be in the $1 million-plus range. In a contributory negligence state, this could be an all-or-nothing factor. Case evaluation software will have a difficult time accounting for this difference.

Like it or not, analytical computerized claim valuation tools are here to stay. Claim professionals who are knowledgeable about the products, their strengths and limitations, can effectively use them as both a sword and shield to successfully defend insurance claims.

Ten Ways to Avoid a Runaway Jury Award

1. Hire the best defense attorney. Pay for quality and cry only once.
2. Realistically evaluate settlement before trial.
3. Do not become ego- or emotionally invested in your own reserve or valuation number.
4. Be alert to late-breaking pretrial developments that can materially impact claim value.
5. Settle!! Pursue alternate dispute resolution forums—such as settlement conferences, mediation, and mini-trials.
6. Round-table the case's settlement value with various defense counsel and with other peer claim professionals.
7. Use computerized claim valuation tools as reality checks or sounding boards.
8. During trial, be attuned to listening between the lines for factors that might justify a reevaluation of the case or of settlement opportunities.
9. During trial, always be thinking, "Do we have grounds for appeal or reversible error if the jury goes crazy?"
10. If a jury award runs rampant, seek a J.N.O.V. Pursue a vigorous appeal.

CHAPTER 4

Delivering Bad News

. . .without getting torched

Here you go again. Your nickname around the office—only half jokingly—is The Grim Reaper, and it's not because you dress in Goth garb. When you appear, bad news seems to follow. (Where did you put your black hood and scythe? Does that qualify as business casual?)

Does life seem to rain on the adjuster's parade? Let us count some of the ways it can. The claim took a turn for the worse. The reserve needs to be bumped up. The client is upset. The attorney's bill was five times what you expected. Your company just got sued for bad faith. Your key person just quit. The jury socked you with a big award.

Let's face it, you rarely grace anyone's doorway, especially the boss's, with good news. When higher-ups hear from you it's because some of the bad stuff hit the fan. The boss is starting to associate you with a dark cloud. Also, the boss does not always react well to bad news. You have to pick and choose your spots with care. Timing is crucial.

Now you've got some more bad news. No point in keeping it all bottled up. Time to spread the cheer and sunshine. Let people start calling your claims unit, The Bad News Bearers.

The challenge here is—how do you deliver bad news to the boss and still keep your head, your job, and your sanity? What will you do?

Don't Be a Dan Rather

One thing not to do is see yourself solely as a communicator.

"Don't `Dan Rather' me!"

That's the admonishment for adjusters who simply bring me bad news with no suggested solutions or action plan. Dan Rather does that, and I might add he gets paid a nice sum to do so. He simply reports the news. He reports on famine, flood, war, terrorism and global warming. He offers solace and consolation but no solutions for these problems, nor do we expect him to.

That's his job description, not yours. More is expected from you. Delivering bad news without getting your head lopped off is an art form. Few (if any) are born with this skill—it must be acquired. The aim here is to help you learn it.

Are you Dan Rather with regard to your boss? Is your adjusting staff a group of Dan Rathers? Do they bring bad news with no idea of solutions? Hopefully not. If they are, you need to break them—and yourself—of any Dan Rather tendencies.

Honing Delivery Skills

One key step is to be seen as part of the solution, not just part of the problem. We should expect claim professionals to go the extra mile in not only reporting bad news but also in adding a suggestion or two on how to address it, how to manage the situation, or how to contain the damage.

Assess your own communication style, especially with higher ups. Do you do an information dump, where you disgorge the bad news with no recommended action? This could include:

- "The claim just doubled in value."

- "Our attorney found some damaging documents in the insured's records."

- "A turncoat employee is helping the plaintiff attorney."

- "The jury came back, and the punitive award is $5 million."

- "The special damages are double what we had estimated."

- "The plaintiff just hired Johnny Cochran as his lawyer."

- "The insured has filed for bankruptcy."

- "The insured's product has had a recall."

- "Our expert's deposition went poorly."

- "Our best adjuster just quit and we have no imminent replacement prospects."

- "The policyholder threatens to drop us if we don't (fill in the blank) pay this claim, use this attorney, try this case, etc."

- "The plaintiff makes so sympathetic an appearance that Ebenezer Scrooge would weep at her testimony."

As claim professionals, we continually face (even if we do not invite) such Maalox moments. They come with the job. If we cannot deal with this, then we are likely in the wrong business. I joke with clients that, "If your company name doesn't ring a bell, consider it a compliment. The only reason you and I would be on a first-name basis is if you have lots of claims, which is the opposite of what both of us want!"

The preceding list is just a sampling of the bad news that adjusters receive and that we are called upon to deliver occasionally. The delivery person does what I call a data vomit—disgorging lots of information and feeling better after doing it. It's akin to taking that monkey off your back and putting it on someone else's shoulder. Nice try! Don't let it happen.

Who's Got the Monkey?

Who's got the monkey in your company, your claims department or work team?

If you're a boss (e.g., claim manager, supervisor, team leader) who collects monkeys, you have a problem. So what will you do about it? Maybe you can . . .

- Alert your reinsurer to the claim that doubled in value.

- Move quickly to settle a claim with bad documents.

- Seek a restraining order on the turncoat employee.

- File a declaratory action to exclude coverage of the punitive award if the policy warrants it.

- Audit the added special damages to see how soft they are.

- Exploit Johnny Cochran's mixed popularity among many who associate him with O.J. Simpson's slick legal defense.

- Use the bankruptcy as a way to either stay litigation against the insured or leverage it for a pennies-on-the-dollar settlement (turn lemons into lemonade!).

- File a motion in limine to exclude evidence of a recall coming before a jury.

- Hire a new expert or better prep the expert before she appears at trial.

- Bifurcate a trial on liability and damages so that, if you are judged to be liable, you can decide then whether to settle the claim or allow the jury to see the sympathetic plaintiff.

These are just some examples of action items and remedies that adjusters may consider in response to various bits of bad news.

Moral: Don't just bring problems and bad news. Bring solutions. Even if it's a half-baked solution, it's better than having no solution at all. It shows initiative and you immediately shift the focus of the discussion to a constructive, problem-solving plane. Believe me, you'd much rather be there than wallowing in the muck of "How bad it is."

Do you really want to be a Dan Rather?

I'd rather not. And I'd rather that you not be one, either.

Other advice in dealing with bad news delivery includes the following items.

Steel Yourself to Not Procrastinate

If you put things off, you better own stock in the company that makes Rolaids®. Inherent in claims work are annoying and anxiety-producing tasks. All of these involve elements of delivering bad news or doing distasteful things, such as

- returning phone calls of jerks,

- taking unpopular positions,

- explaining exclusions to someone who thought they had "full coverage,"

- finishing a project under a tight deadline, or

- giving the boss bad news about a trial that was lost.

These are tempting to put off.

DON'T!!

Delay in facing these only worsens the situation: your anxiety increases. The problem festers.

An old Nike ad campaign featured the tag line, "Just do it."

Let's modify that. When delivering bad news, "Do it *now!*" To paraphrase a quip about aged claims, "Bad news, unlike fine wine, does not improve with age."

Choose Solution-minded Team Members

If you're a claims manager, choose your claims team and associates (and team members) with care so that they are not afraid to bring bad news to you. Hire people who think positively, even in the face of adversity. This is tough, because there is so much adversity in claims work. Avoid complainers and whiners. Ever been around people who constantly complain?

Remember Doug & Wendy Whiner and their pity parties from the old *Saturday Night Live* shows?

Avoid pity parties! After a half-hour of them, your energy is drained by the negative stress they bring.

The key lies in asking complainers: Can you control the situation you're complaining about?

If so, change things!

If not, stop complaining because it won't do any good.

Be Proactive

It's best for higher-ups to hear bad news from you. This way, there will be no suspicion that you are suppressing things. Also, you get a chance to put your spin on the situation (some might decry spin control). In any event, the best way to manage the problem is to get on top of it early, long before it grows into an 800-pound gorilla. You never want the boss to hear the bad news from someone else. You never want the boss thinking, "I wonder what *else* is happening in his department that I should know about." This line of thinking is rarely productive for your advancement chances if they apply to you. Take ownership, take accountability, and take charge.

Hold Service Providers Accountable

Don't let service providers become Dan Rathers, either. Here's an infuriating situation. My defense attorney comes to me the day before trial. She reports some eleventh-hour adverse development. A former employee of the insured has just gone over to the dark side. Some smoking gun document has surfaced. The plaintiff's expert says that the future loss of earnings will be astronomical. The attorney regurgitates all this and asks me what I want to do.

What do *I* want to do? Arrrgh! Right now, I'd like to jump off a bridge. For this I'm paying $150 per hour.

Here is what is much preferable. The attorney reports that the problem. The reason we are learning about it so late is (fill in the blank). The impact on the case value could be (fill in the blank).

"Here are our options and what we can do about this: 1, 2, 3 ..."

"Here is what I recommend and why:"

"Please let me know what you would like to do. We will need to decide by XXXX. I will follow up with a phone call once you've had a little bit of time to digest this..."

This is much preferable to dumping a problem in my lap and plaintively asking, "What do you want to do?"

The second approach provides some context, identifies options, and shows that the attorney has done her homework. She seems to be part of the solution, not part of the problem. There is no sense of panic on her part. She has digested the developments and has laid out the options in a businesslike manner. Each option has pros and cons. She sticks her neck out by making a recommendation, but she also acknowledges that the final decision is mine. She lets me know how much or how little time we have to decide. Finally, she promises to call me and does NOT ask me to call her, a nice touch since I am the one paying the bill. (Memo to service providers—if I'm paying your bill, you call me—do not send me an email saying, "Please call me." If I'm the client, you chase me.)

Follow this example when you're the one who has to deliver bad news. Make sure you bring some solutions with you.

An occupational hazard in communicating not only bad news but also potentially bad news is that you may end up dropping flares over situations that do not materialize into major problems. In fact, it may get to the point where you seem to be an alarmist Chicken Little, always squawking, "The sky is falling!"

To a degree, this is an occupational hazard. It is probably better to err on the side of over-communicating when it comes to bad news or potential negative developments. Again, avoid having higher-ups asking or thinking, "Why didn't we see this coming?" or asking, "How long have you known about this?" Better to be perceived as a Chicken Little than to be seen as one who sweeps negative situations under the rug.

Set a good example here for your staff. Make sure that **you** do not kill the messenger when your reports bring you unwelcome news. Model the kind of behavior you would hope to get from your boss. Do you feel annoyance when one of your reports brings you bad news? Do you ever take it out on staff members? If there are implicit penalties for bringing the boss bad news, there's a good chance the boss will only find out about bad situations when they are too far advanced to be fixed.

The point: earlier is better in terms of getting word of a bad situation. The ability to redirect the situation grows if you can get to problems early on. The challenge is that no one likes to be the one to bring bad news to the boss, even if the boss accepts such news with serenity.

Pointers from the Field

Lyle Walker, President of Walker Risk Management in Allen Park, Michigan, states:

> Do not put off telling whoever has to be apprised. Second, tell it all in one summary sentence. Then, if your audience still accepts your existence, provide the necessary detail. Always state in some way that you just learned about the situation and wanted to advise them right away, although some further developments may change the picture. Emphasize how quickly you got to them about the subject. Then buy a newspaper and check the "Help Wanted" ads.

William C. Strachan, ARM, Risk Manager, Town of Enfield, Connecticut, states that bad news should not be delivered after the fact. Groundwork should be laid so that the potential was known. Any suggestion to prevent the bad outcome should be developed and implemented. He notes, "Bosses always HATE surprises!!!! Stay on top of the situation and keep them informed." He concludes with a warning, "Messengers do get shot!"

Charles Chaffin of Chary Consultants, Inc., of Macon, Georgia, says that claims people have challenges that go beyond being the bearers of bad news. The problem is that clients often think they know more about claims that the professional adjusters who handle losses for a living.

> The problem is insurance. Most people feel they don't have the right kind of insurance or what they have is too expensive. Invariably, they have a buddy in the business telling them why the risk manager is doing everything wrong. Add to that, they may have picked up a few buzz words and think they know everything about insurance.

> When an event occurs, they want it to be disregarded. "No need to investigate as it makes us look like we did something wrong."

Those that see loss runs always say that the reserves are too high, that the claim is not worth that. The real hot spot, however, is when the time comes to settle a claim. They want to defend it to the Supreme Court.

Thirteen Tips for Delivering Bad News and Still Keeping Your Job

1. Focus not just on claim problems but also on solutions.
2. Don't report any claim problem to the boss without being prepared to recommend solutions.
3. Identify the options available. Think of at least three.
4. Lay out the pros and cons of each option.
5. Offer your recommendation, or be prepared to if asked.
6. Turn the dialogue about problems into one of joint collaboration.
7. Indicate to the boss or client the time-sensitivity of the matter.
8. Appraise the communication style of your claim staff—especially your direct reports. Train them to adopt this approach with you.
9. Encourage independent problem solving with your staff. Encourage them to alert you to problems proactively but not to just do a hit-and-run information dump.
10. Seek opportunities to spread a little sunshine and good news, such as claim dismissals, trial wins, excellent settlements, successful motions for summary judgment, complimentary letters or feedback from happy customers, or one of your adjusters passing an insurance exam or getting a designation.
11. Encourage your team to bring you problems—or potential problems—early on.
12. In delivering bad news, the mantra should be, "Tell it all, tell it fast, and tell the truth."
13. Time is of the essence. The problem will not improve with age. The longer you wait between the claims crisis and delivering the news, the more time exists for misinformation, rumors, or panic to spread.

CHAPTER 5

Ready, Aim, Fire . . .

You're fired or laid off

You've turned it over in your mind again and again. You didn't see it coming. Your performance evaluations were fine. Work life seemed to be clicking along nicely. Today the boss dropped the bombshell, though. Due to corporate financial performance and orders from on high, you're being laid off. Sorry—it's nothing personal. Many thanks for your time here. You'll have one week of severance pay for each year worked. Please box up your personal effects and turn in your security pass card to Human Resources. No hard feelings and . . . good luck!

What will you do?

Surviving a layoff is a key component for the adjuster's personal and career risk management. In many organizations, the claims function is viewed as expendable. We've all heard the knocks on claims. They are a black hole that swallows money. They are a cost center. Companies trying to turn around their business fortunes will hire more sales people and underwriters but rarely more claims people. For whatever reason, claims people may be vulnerable to the last hired-first fired phenomenon.

Some (many?) organizations facing tough economic times may view the claims staff (or your position) as a dispensable frill. Like it or not, this occurs. People who choose this profession must face this reality with open eyes.

As painful as it is to realize, the general business and economic layoff phenomenon impacts claim professionals and makes them vulnerable to the prospect of pink slips. Claims work is not recession-proof, unfortunately. Charity begins at home, and personal risk management should start with the claims professional taking specific steps to stave off this eventuality and plan for the unthinkable.

One obvious suggestion: Constantly add value to your department, work team, and organization, making yourself as indispensable as possible. Building bridges within the organization with a cooperative attitude and a strong sense of internal customers is vital.

Despite the best plans, though, claim professionals can still find themselves the victims of corporate layoffs or firings. Here are some tips on how to manage that personal (and personnel) risk..

One key premise of career management is to pack one's survival gear long before the employment floor gives way: Dig your well before you're thirsty. The era of lifetime employment—within claims or in any realm—is over. Sudden changes in business conditions, company profitability, or personnel changes at the very top can challenge your status as an employed claims professional. How do you deal with that risk, that worst-case scenario? This chapter offers some practical tips for claim professionals to manage such career risks.

Seek Severance

It never hurts to ask. Some companies may be in a generous (or guilty) frame of mind when they let you go. Capitalize on this by seeking the best possible severance package you can get. This will give you a longer financial bridge while you seek subsequent employment. One reason you want and need the largest severance package available is because it takes more time these days than in the past to find another job. According to the Bureau of Labor Statistics, it now takes job hunters an average of 9.6 weeks to find replacement work, as compared to 5.8 weeks in the early 1990s ("Driving the SUV to the Food Pantry," Business *Week*, 4/28/03.)

Don't Debate

You are unlikely to argue your way back onto the company rolls. No matter how shocked you are, hold your fire and bite your tongue. Do not grovel, beg, or plead for your job. This has a zero chance of succeeding. Sympathy may exist but has its limits. Companies do not keep people on their payroll out of pity. If the company has decided to terminate you, an impassioned plea will not make it reverse course. Preserve your dignity. If you have any arguments, hold them in reserve for a forum where they can be weighed more dispassionately.

By other arguments, we mean to matters such as sexual harassment; age, gender, or racial discrimination; and retaliation for uncovering wrong-doing. If you feel you are being terminated for reasons such as these, seek the advice of legal counsel to see if you have a viable cause of action. You may not get reinstated, but you may be entitled to damages that can offer a financial lifeline as you work to find subsequent employment and get back on your feet.

Be a Super Saver

Many observers view Americans as poor savers. Those who have little or no financial margin are exquisitely vulnerable to financial devastation from layoffs. **Solution:** start building a rainy day fund, even if you feel your current job situation is bulletproof. Buck the spend and debt trend as a hedge against layoffs that may affect your tenure as an employed claims professional. Many experts suggest that you squirrel away enough cash to get by for at least three months without a paycheck. Six months might be better. Formulate a personal budget and review it with a magnifying glass to determine how to squeeze extra savings to funnel into this fund.

Go On a Debt Diet

Do not prepay lower cost debt such as car loans or mortgages until you have the rest of your finances under control. First priority—build cash reserves. Then, pay off high interest charge and credit cards. Then, raise the maximum amount to pay for retirement savings. Then start pre-paying low-cost loans.

If you are laid off from a claims position, avoid using savings or severance to liquidate your debt—even high interest rate credit card debt. Make only the minimum payments until you are back on a payroll.

Assess 401(k) Participation

If you have access to a 401(k) plan and your employer matches your contributions, contribute at least as much to earn the maximum match. If you have little or no emergency cash, though, save the money even if it means reducing your 401(k) contribution.

Manage Health Benefits

Those claim professionals who handle employee benefits should be conversant with provisions of the Consolidated Omnibus Budget Reconciliation Act of 1986 (COBRA). By way of review: if you are laid off, COBRA rules let you keep your group plan for eighteen months—at your expense—if your company employs twenty or more people. You must, however, apply within sixty days of termination. Working couples may find it cheaper to buy family coverage under a spouse's plan. **Caveat:** make sure your spouse's plan does not exclude coverage for recurrence of past illnesses or conditions.

Leave Retirement Funds Alone

If you become a laid-off claims person, do not drain cash out of your 401(k), even small amounts. Withdrawals carry the double whammy of taxes and a 10 percent penalty. Further, you lose a valuable tax deferral.

If your layoff lasts long, you might need some of your retirement money to help pay bills. Draw only a modest amount out per month, though.

File for unemployment compensation benefits. These, combined with severance, may help tide you over financially while looking for a new job, whether that new job happens to be within or outside the claims field.

Advice from the Field

Consider Self-employment

Barry Zalma, an insurance attorney from Culver City, California, says,

Either start an independent adjusting company or find a new job. Not a real problem if I'm as good as I think. If not, if I was worthy of being laid off, I would live off the dole, relatives, and friends until I was forced on some unsuspecting yet stupid employer.

Beaumont Vance, risk manager for Sun Microsystems in Broomfield, Colorado, says,

Contact a claims temp agency, negotiate a severance package in exchange for a waiver, and network your brains out, especially with brokers.

Reevaluate Career Goals and Career Change Options

Nancy Germond, President of The Insurance Writer in Jefferson City, Missouri, suggests:

Consider a career change. After almost twenty years in this industry, with two parents and one brother who spent a combined 105 years or more in the industry, I can safely say it "ain't the industry it used to be." Nor do I think it ever will be again.

Anyone laid off in this market should take a long, hard look at what they are truly happy doing. Forget about the money, forget the golden handcuffs of security such as health coverage (take advantage of COBRA), and change careers. If you're truly happy in this industry, great. If there's the least bit of doubt, spread your wings and fly (or crash land and then look for an insurance job).

Lyle Walker, President of Walker Risk Management in Allen Park, Michigan offers four rules for playing—and winning—the layoff game:

One: Always keep track of where your organization is going and its financials. Early alert to what might happen gives greater time to do something about it. (In my case I did exactly that, knew with a degree of certainty I was to be restrategized, and was some prepared for when it happened).

Two: Always, from the day you are employed, think about your next job. How is your present employment preparing you for this next job? How are you preparing yourself for this next job through training and/or education? How prepared are you, always, to make a change in employment before or after being let go? (I was structured to take early retirement, which I in fact did)

Three: Always think the person you are working for is yourself! Always think that you are working for money that you will use to satisfy the needs and wants of yourself and family. You may have what is called an employer, but in fact you work for yourself.

Four: Always observe what is being rewarded in your present employment and in other places. As an employee, direct your activities to those things being rewarded to maximize your income, regardless of whether such rewards are in the interests of the company objectives (that's management's responsibility). However, when rewards and company objectives do not coincide, start looking for other employment, as your present job will collapse soon if not a little way down the line.

This sounds cynical and contrary to the loyalty employees are supposed to show. This runs counter to how I was raised. The world changes, however, and the above is simply a statement of fact as I see it today.

Another claims person, requesting anonymity, writes,

Your mom's advice, "Reap what you sow," was never more true. Adjusters who epitomize the "Me first" reputation, use Mary Carter deals, lack integrity, and otherwise fail to manifest reasonable standards learn those traits do not open doors.

I attended outplacement counseling as part of a package for senior staff when a medical malpractice mutual closed a regional office and I did not wish to move to Las Vegas. The weekly sessions invariably included advice to mine the Rolodex. Some statistics were cited, and they overwhelmingly supported the idea that most future job offers to the downsized came from prior contacts.

One statement was, "You already know your next boss, and you likely will be surprised."

It's another chapter in the story of the squirrel burying acorns in the summer. Good habits you practice (fair deals, staying current in your profession, long hours, helping others) are like the nuts for winter; the best chance you have for your future.

Loan Receipt Agreements, a/k/a "Mary Carter"

One controversial settlement technique is the *loan receipt agreement,* commonly referred to as a "Mary Carter" agreement, first reported in the case of *Booth v. Mary Carter Paint Co.,* 202 So.2d 8 (Fla. Dist. Ct. App. 1967). A loan receipt agreement is an agreement between the plaintiff and one or more defendants in which a settling defendant(s) "loan(s)" a stated sum of money to the plaintiff and is entitled to be repaid the loan from any recovery the plaintiff receives from a nonsettling defendant. *Banovz v. Rantanen,* 649 N.E. 2d 977 (Ill. App. Ct. 1995). The essential feature of a "Mary Carter" agreement is the repayment of the loan from monies recovered from the nonsettling codefendants. *Banovz* at 622. Should there be no further recovery, there is no repayment.

Regina Berens, an actuary with Employers Re in Overland Park, Kansas offers the following advice:

1. **Be candid with your support network.** Tell the truth to the people who care about you. When I was let go from a job in 1995, my son was eleven. I told him the truth, contrary to the advice of the outplacement firm. Children learn from their parents how to handle life's setbacks.

2. **Beware of working through multiple recruiters.** If you decide to work with multiple recruiters, tell them the ground rules: "Do not send my name to a company without my okay in advance." Get it in writing. The last thing you want is two recruiters sending your resume to the same place and then arguing over who gets the fee. I'm sorry to say that in my last job search, even though everyone agreed to this in advance and I kept careful records of who sent my credentials where, my name ended up in one place through four people. If you plan to approach a company on your own, tell the recruiter so he does not send your resume there. To be fair, do not tell Recruiter A where Recruiter B sent you if Recruiter B was unaware of the opening. You're giving away Recruiter A's hard work to the competitor.

3. **Always have lots of irons in the fire.** In my last job search, I never had a day when every lead had been closed. There was always a place that hadn't answered yet.

4. **Don't give up hope.** I've seen really good people take nine months to a year to find another position. Two of them landed in good positions without relocating. Not a great scenario, but better than a lifetime sentence of, "Do you want paper or plastic?" I was in a high-priority job search a year ago and in the last couple of months have gotten calls from recruiters with positions that just opened up.

Berens offers other strategies:

1. **Live within your means.** When things got tight, I wasn't able to save money, but at least I could keep my son in the private school where he was thriving.

2. **Get a home equity line of credit if things look shaky.** This is not a loan—just the ability to borrow if you need it. I never touched mine but was very glad it was there.

3. **Network, network, network.** Keep in touch with colleagues who moved elsewhere even if it's only an email every six months or so. Plenty of people have called to pick my brain during job searches. While I've never been able to directly get anyone hired, I like to think that I helped keep some individuals sane enough to make the next phone call or send the next resume.

Phil Bly is the Director of Risk Management for Crescent Heights of America, Inc., (Miami). He notes that, unfortunately, he has lots of personal experience in this area. His first pink slip was in 1974 due to the mid-70s hard market. Black Friday, he recalls, saw 500 people get the axe. "My three years got me two weeks severance," Bly adds. Fortunately, his boss had already arranged a new position for him at another insurer.

Bly observes that many people have a financial plan associated with "dying tomorrow." Losing one's job is not real different, he believes. From his personal experience, Bly offers the following survival tips:

1. Never let yourself think you can't be replaced.

2. Never let yourself think that your employer actually cares about you. You're gone in sixty seconds when things go bad.

3. Always be looking at other opportunities. For me, it's the RIMS Job Bank and other sites like Monster and CareerBuilder. Apply for positions that look interesting and go to interviews if for no other reason than to stay in practice.

4. Don't let misguided loyalty hold you back from a better opportunity.

5. Maintain a network.

6. Don't let anyone convince you that answering employment ads is a waste of time. My nine jobs were obtained by (A) personal referrals, (B) prospecting potential employers, and (C) responding to job ads.

7. Live within your means. If you spend more than you make and use credit cards to finance your lifestyle, you're in trouble when paychecks stop.

8. Never decline an interview. The only thing you turn down is an offer.

9. Apply for jobs in your field, even if you don't have the qualifications listed. Sometimes, the successful candidate is not the most qualified. My current employer had a specific requirement for background in high-rise construction—which I don't have—yet here I am.

10. If you think you have a basis for a lawsuit against the former employer, go for it.

11. Apply for unemployment. You can do this online in many states and not have to stand in line.

12. If you are very cash-strapped and you are offered outplacement, consider taking the cash that the employer plans to spend on this service. It can help to have someplace to go everyday and use someone else's resources, but from my own experience the real value of outplacement is suspect.

Some Unemployment Facts

If you resign, you may be denied unemployment benefits, regardless of the reason for your departure (e.g., job stress was slowly killing you). The employer may well win.

Tips:

Do not resign.

Before buying anything ask yourself, "Could I sell this on e-Bay for what I am paying for it or maybe more?" If you can't say yes, then you probably don't need it.

Don't believe in debt reduction schemes and work-at-home emails. Many of these are scams.

Other survival tips if you happen to find yourself a victim of a layoff include:

1. Understand the severance agreement before you sign it. Don't hurry—take your time to make sure you understand it. Get legal assistance if needed.

2. Absent union regulations or an employment contract, an employer is not obligated to pay severance.

3. Do not be ashamed to talk to colleagues and friends. Tap into your resource network for emotional support. Build your support network long before any crisis arrives—dig your well before you are thirsty!

4.   If the company offers any outplacement assistance and you have a cash cushion to carry your living expenses for a few months, take advantage of it. If it is not offered, try to negotiate that as part of your severance package.

Resources that May Be Downloaded from the Internet for Those Laid Off

Two brief resources are available on surviving layoffs. Both are available from Amazon.com for a modest price:

Empty Cubicles: Employee Retention When Downsizing — Avoid The Anxiety Created By Layoffs [DOWNLOAD: PDF] by Beverly Goldberg (Author), $3.25

Work 2.5: How to Survive the Next Layoffs [DOWNLOAD: PDF] by Bill Jensen (Author) $2.95 Edition: e-book (Acrobat Reader)

CHAPTER 6

They Vote with Their Feet

Your best adjuster just quit

Your best claims person—the one who handles the toughest files, shoulders the highest caseload, has the best relations with key clients, is the go-to person on tough assignments—just gave you two weeks notice. There goes your day, as well as your peace of mind. And you thought this was going to be an easy day at the old claims office!

Your mind reels from the shock. You feel a mixture of betrayal and panic. Why didn't you see this coming? You thought things were copasetic. You really don't have the luxury of licking your wounded feelings in an orgy of self-pity, though. Your immediate worry—what to do with the caseload that will suddenly need new ownership in two weeks.

The clock is ticking. You're under the gun. Your palms start to sweat. You can't forget that corporate is currently under a big cost-cutting initiative. You wonder if you'll even be given clearance to hire a replacement. If you are permitted to hire someone, how long will it take to replace your key person? Where did you put that bottle of anti-acids?

How do you respond when your key claims person resigns? What will you do?

Handling an Unexpected Vacancy

Carve Out Time

First off, hit the pause button on your daily schedule. Whatever you're doing, drop it. Make time to meet with the person who just gave notice and talk with him. This has priority over everything else. You need to find out more. Give your staff standing orders that you must be notified *immediately* if any of your staff gives notice.

Unfortunately, we often tend to take top performers for granted. Show that talking with the individual who has resigned is a top priority on your daily work schedule and agenda.

Find Out Why

Get a grip on your emotions. Your reaction may include intense shock, anger, disappointment, panic, or betrayal. Control your feelings and don't let them seep through. Go to the person with the idea of listening more than talking.

Are they leaving for money? Benefits? Because of friction with coworkers? Troublesome clients? Workload issues? Compatibility with you, the boss? Personal reasons?

Address the Reasons

Maybe it's too late, but perhaps not. If the problem is salary, can you match the offer? If the problem is workload, can you redistribute it? The painful truth is that the employee may be giving you feedback that you need to hear. If the employee is worth keeping, she is worth fighting for. If the demands are not exorbitant and if you don't feel that you're being taken advantage of, consider what you can do, what you can change to get the employee to reconsider. If the commute has become intolerable, how about a flextime arrangement or a telecommuting option one day a week?

Admittedly, none of this is guaranteed to make the person stay, but it's worth a try. If you do nothing, it's guaranteed that she will leave. So the issue is—do you even try or do you let her just walk out the door? Try!!

Know When to Stop

You've identified the reasons why your best adjuster is leaving. You've made inducements to get her to stay—better pay, a promotion, a transfer, a more manageable caseload. Despite your best efforts, there is no changing her mind. She is determined to leave.

Persistence is a virtue but, at some point, recognize reality and quit trying to lobby. After a point, it becomes humiliating. Respect the decision of the person leaving and work with her in the intervening time to effectuate a smooth transition. Get beyond the shock, the hurt and disappointment. Console yourself by knowing that you did your best to keep a good employee.

Cultivate the Equivalent of a Farm Team

Diversify your talent base. Do not put all of your eggs in one talent pool basket. Barry Zalma, an attorney from Culver City, California, who specializes in insurance claims states,

> If your best adjuster suddenly quits, it is too late. An intelligent claims department has a team of people who are trained, continuously to do good work and work with that best claims person to become better or as good as the best claims person. If that is the case, when one resigns the next can move up from the farm system. If you don't have a professional department, be afraid, be very afraid.

G. Craig Thummel is a risk management consultant from Houston. He cautions that:

> Two weeks is not a crisis. No notice might be. Conduct an immediate exit interview to determine why. Don't attempt to salvage, and wish him well. In the remote event the person truly does not want to leave maybe something can be worked out. However, something like 75 percent of those so salvaged end up leaving within a year anyway.

How do you deal with your internal staff as you try to plug the holes? Here are some suggestions.

1. Communicate immediately with internal staff and tell them how you will manage the transition so they don't have to imagine what will happen and how they might be affected.

2. Work with claim unit members to develop a transition plan that identifies all affected stakeholders and addresses their needs.

3. Communicate the change and interim actions to all stakeholders. Tailor the message to each. Collect their buy-in and feedback.

4. Work with the key person to inventory and prioritize the caseload and make assignments.

5. Schedule briefing sessions with those inheriting files.

6. Develop a follow-through plan so important cases and related issues get handled and your staff remains confident in your support for them. Recognize their efforts and accomplishments.

7. Have a great party for the departing person.

8. Work out a longer term staffing plan and look hard at what you just learned, if anything.

Some observers are skeptical toward the theory that more money is the answer to adjuster retention problems. David P. Broussard, CIC, CRM, CWCP, manager of underwriting services for Amerisafe, Inc., DeRidder, Louisiana, says that throwing more money at him is only a short-term fix. In many cases, it addresses the symptom, not the problem. Without changing the way things are done and fixing the real reasons for leaving, he will be gone eventually anyway.

Consultant Thummel says,

Statistically, a huge percent (about 75 percent) of those so enticed to stay end up leaving within a year anyway. It's usually not about the money, so—in the end—the real reasons win out unless they are addressed.

Thomas Bower of the New York City law firm of Shaub Ahmuty Citrin & Spratt, LLP, says,

> If they've already decided to leave and you offer them more money, they'll just use that to negotiate an even higher starting salary with the new employer. I've seen that used as a deliberate tactic more than once. Although people usually won't leave unless they can get more money elsewhere, it's not the money that makes them look in the first place.

Look at the root cause of turnover, especially when a valued adjuster gives notice. For example, some observers feel that many employee retention plans are lifeboat drills. After the *Abandon Ship* horn blares, management and the Human Resources department initiate drills to retain the nearly departed. Often, these efforts only succeed in keeping those whose resignations were no more than a negotiation ploy.

The time to retain key employees is early, before they begin to look elsewhere. Stay tuned to your employees' needs.

Unfortunately, it is sad but true that some corporate policies seem perversely designed to force good claims people out. Examples:

1.　Use it or lose it vacation accruals that hurt older workers who need to bank time in case of illness.

2.　Reaching a maximum salary level for a given job. Why *not* leave for more pay?

3.　Mindless Dilbert-esque strategies that afflict the claims business, convincing employees that they are trapped in a cartoon:

   •　"Keep expenses under 25 percent." (Hey, try reducing indemnity expenses!)

   •　"Close 10 percent of your files a month." (No matter how much more you have to pay?)

   •　"Telephone interviews are cheaper." (Yes, but shouldn't we care about fraud?)

Nancy Germond of The Insurance Writer (Jefferson City, Missouri) states,

> If proper exit interviews are conducted when employees leave and are acted upon, a lot fewer people would be looking for jobs. Most organizations have someone in personnel conduct the exit interview. Unfortunately, the results often are left in a drawer somewhere. Top management should ensure that the proper person, who understands the department and issues the employee is fleeing, conduct the interview. It must be reviewed by top management, and remedial fixes must be made—or at least attempts must be made to get to the truth behind accusations, allegations, or complaints.

She continues,

> I hate when people say it isn't about the money because, when they say that, 99 percent of the time it is about the money. Many times it's also about a lack of respect. I always tell people when they are resigning that, if they are ambivalent about leaving, they have to search their hearts and do what their hearts tell them to do. Many times people don't really want to leave—they just want to feel like someone wants them around and would miss them.

> A great book is *Bowling Alone: The Collapse and Revival of American Community* by Robert D. Putnam (New York: Simon & Schuster, 2000), which talks about the breakdown of social support in the U.S. People used to belong to bowling leagues, square dancing, Rotary, the Kiwanis, a church, etc. This is not as true anymore.

> The workplace today is one of our focal social ties. Employers can build on that to our advantage if we keep in mind that we all bring our childhood stuff (most of us, that is) to the workplace, and the workplace often becomes like an extended family.

Bruce Higgins, President of B. W Higgins Inc. of Indianapolis, Indiana, an insurance recruiter and placement specialist, says,

Over the years, I have moved many disgruntled and happy employees. I believe I've served both company and candidate in bringing about a more perfect union. The reason is a combination of money, people, places, or perceived company respect for the individual. Pick any two or more. Even the truly happy will consider a move for the right situation that promises to make an area of concern more palatable.

Truth is, career changes are inevitable and, largely to a person, everyone has an invisible chink in the armor of loyalty and longevity that they wear for their employers. Research shows that the average turnover in our industry is 3 1/2 years. While some companies represent the best place to work in the U.S., even they are exposed to the problem.

Truly successful employers face the fact that succession planning is inordinately important to maintain their operation. . .top to bottom. At every department level, managers must be aware of their human assets, how to protect them and, more significantly, how to respond if they can't.

Doing what a company can—to engender pleasant surroundings, a formidable benefit package, and an opportunity for advancement—is necessary. This serves to decrease employee discontent and turnover, but the mover will still move. And the mover can be your best.

Countering employee demand for more money? If they accept, the initial feelings don't go away.... they are just quieted for a period. Even the company has misgivings. "If Jim decides to leave again, can we afford to keep him? Should we give him those added responsibilities that will make him privy to our next marketing roll-out?" Realistically, the counteroffer tends to only support what the employee initially felt. Empowered, a very, very high percentage of those accepting a counteroffer begin looking, avowing not to make the acceptance mistake again.

Brad Webb of Texas Claims & Consulting Services, Inc., in Dallas says

The first thing I recommend after a key employee resigns is to out-source all you can temporarily. This takes the pressure off the remaining staff and lets them absorb the work until you can hire someone to fill the void. Frequently, though, we are working at capacity and I end up giving my (TPA) competition business by suggesting it.

Also, become familiar with senior adjusting staff (catastrophic claim adjusters, litigation specialists, and supervisors from other companies who may be nearing retirement). You need to know where these people can be located after retirement. Many of them will welcome a temporary job six months or more into their retirement when they discover they are bored and broke. They make great temps and—if you can figure out a way to hire them as temporary employees—you can save the 40 to 60 percent fee from agencies.

Offering more money seldom works because any good person will have business ethics and won't renege on accepting an offer from the new company. They are also usually unhappy about some or many things where they have been working. They either need to get out or at least want to try something else.

Often, adjusters leave jobs because of lack of respect, but often it also is about a ton of other things. The social twist is very interesting and very true. Today, we do tend to look to our workplace for social acceptance. You can see this in new employee training classes, where the one who doesn't fit in is the first to leave the company. The same cliques apply as in high school. A bad encounter on a personal level can make a great day horrible very quickly. It can also be the last straw for someone who just doesn't like the job or was a bad job match.

Having said that, money does play a role. Most people don't work simply because they enjoy getting up every morning and driving into the office. They work to make a living. Money can be the deciding factor. New friends can be made, especially if an employee does not have a long tenure with the company.

Much also hinges on the company as a whole. Did someone in Human Resources not offer to help when an employee's health insurance deduction was wrong? Did the supervisor miscalculate vacation time and did it take three months to correct it? Seemingly small problems can pile up and make someone look for greener pastures elsewhere.

In other cases, the departing employees are smart. They know their job, and they begin to look to see if they are getting paid for what they are worth.

Often, the breakdown is from management being focused only on profits and pushing as much work as possible to an ever-smaller pool of employees. They are busy trying to implement changes that may or may not make efficient and effective use of personnel and resources, but change is good.

One useful practice is to have ex-employees interviewed by qualified interviewers three to six months after leaving. This can accomplish several things. First employees have had a chance to review and compare their old jobs with the new so can give real insight into why they left. They know they will be staying at the new job, so they no longer have to hedge their exit interview responses by merely saying they got a better opportunity. They can be impartial and blunt, as well as objective about the good and bad aspects of the old job.

Secondly, in the intervening time they may realize they made a mistake. If management wants them back, it may be possible to regain their intellectual capital now that they have some insight from the new company.

George Mullins, who works for a major insurer's special investigative unit based in Birmingham, Alabama, however, believes that:

> It's too late. Let the person go—wish him well—and put in your next best. Truly no one is indispensable. Ripples will happen but the waters will calm. If the shop falls apart—then someone was not watching the entire shop—and it's time to rebuild, including the supervisor.

Twelve Ways to Cope with Your Best Adjuster Leaving

1. Don't take it personally.
2. Immediately initiate a recruitment process.
3. Send him off with class.
4. Part as friends.
5. Have an exit interview and learn from it.
6. Reassure clients.
7. Communicate with the rest of the staff.
8. Decide what to do about caseload coverage.
9. Notify service providers.
10. Don't rush to any conclusions.
11. Consider a temp service as a bridge.
12. Stay in touch.

Patrick J. Vuchetich, general claims manager – environmental for Williams and Company Consulting, Inc., Kansas City, Missouri, offers the following guidelines for preventing good employees from leaving.

Your Best Adjuster Quits: Preventive Checklist

❑ Survey employees periodically for job satisfaction and workplace improvements.

❑ Meet regularly with employees and take their satisfaction temperatures.

❑ Spot-check to gauge satisfaction quotient.

❑ Tell staff, "Don't do anything without first talking to me."

❑ Take care of your strong performers!

❑ Fight for adequate resources, such as salary, benefits, staffing, flex time options, telecommuting options, and equipment.

❑ Be flexible with employee requests about work hours, scheduling, and personal emergencies.

❑ Be attuned to reading signs and tea leaves.

❑ Keep your Rolodex current with information about headhunters and staffing firms.

❑ Have job descriptions and job ads composed and ready to go.

CHAPTER 7

Squeezing the Lemon

Your good claims hire turns
out to be a dud

That new adjuster you hired seemed so bright and promising. The job interviews went well. References checked out nicely. The vibes were good. You were delighted that you got the position filled. Now, you can breathe a sigh of relief and cross that To-Do *off your checklist.*

That was then—this is now. You're starting to have doubts. In the first ninety days, there are problems with attendance and punctuality. He's leaving early and coming in late. Lots of time spent on socializing and chitchat. You seem to be fielding a disproportionate chunk of complaints about the adjuster as well. A recent trial on one of his cases produced a $1 million verdict. Sure, that could happen to anybody, but a later file review revealed that the adjuster gave the case very little work-up, had under-reserved, and had not explored interim settlement opportunities. This doesn't seem to be working out.

What will you do?

Every claims manager or supervisor has occasionally found herself in the position of hiring someone who simply did not work out. When this occurs, how do you handle it? One key first step is to . . .

Implement a Probationary Period

Institute an initial ninety-day probationary period for all new hires, during which you clearly communicate that you can part company for any reason or for no reason at all. You should have a pretty good idea within ninety days as to whether the new employee is a keeper or not. View this as a chance for a mutual employment test drive. If it works out—fine. If it does not work out, no messy divorce is needed.

Despite the most thorough hiring and interviewing process, there are some things you cannot or will not know about a worker until you see her on a sustained day-in day-out basis. It's like the difference between dating and marriage.

Identify the Problem

What exactly is the adjuster's problem? Are there technical shortcomings in claim-handling skills? Does the adjuster understand investigation, coverage, and damage analysis? Are clients complaining? Do the issues relate to work habits—punctuality, attendance, excessive chatting, or fraternization? Is there friction with a coworker or the boss?

Some of these may be corrected through training, coaching, and mentoring. Others, however, may not be so amenable.

If the problems are poor work habits, they may be hard to change. If good work habits are not formed early, they are rarely grafted on later. Work habits include items such as showing up on time; putting in a full day's work; occasionally staying late when the job demands it; and delivering projects, assignments, and deliverables on time. Other factors include more subjective elements of teamwork within the claims department: compatibility with peers; degree of self-motivation; amount of back channel carping and complaining; and chemistry with the boss.

Some organizations say they hire for attitude and train for skill. Southwest Airlines prides itself on this approach. They ask job applicants to tell jokes, do impromptu skits, and demonstrate a sense of humor. It seems to work well for them in the hyper-competitive arena of commercial airlines. This hiring philosophy reflects the idea that skills can be taught; attitude cannot.

Claim managers or supervisors should ponder this. Decide whether the problem is one of skill or one of attitude (or, in the worst case, both). If the attitude is good but the skill is lacking, decide whether you have the time and resources to devote to bringing the employee up to acceptable performance levels. Decide how close they are to acceptable performance and whether it will be a monumental job to train them, outstripping the time and resources you have available.

Of course, the broader question is—how do such candidates slip through to start with? Did they misrepresent their credentials and skills? Were you superficial in the hiring process? Were there early warning signs that could or should have been read and heeded? How can you retool so that a ringer does not slip through again?

When you sense an employee's job performance is deteriorating or simply not reaching the level needed, you need to act quickly and decisively. An initial step is to . . .

Consider Other Reasons

Besides the normal regimen of increased reviews, performance oversight, and the like, consider the possibility of substance abuse as the reason for the poor performance. This is true for newer hires as well as more seasoned employees. A supervisor or manager may surmise two possibilities for a sudden deterioration in performance: substance abuse or personal life problems.

As a manager, first sit down with the troubled employee and ask him point blank what is happening in his personal life. Ask about substance problems. If he denies this, make a clear list of expectations and ways that they will be measured. Then follow up. If either or both alcohol and drugs are a factor, urge the employee to seek professional help. Many employers have employee assistance programs (EAPs) that help address such issues.

The main point is to offer help. Everybody has problems in their lives that compete with work. Rarely does someone engage in this behavior simply because he is a jerk. Something changed between the past good history and the present.

Communicate Concerns

As awkward as it is, do not keep your concerns to yourself. Arrange to meet with the employee in question—in private. Gather your facts in advance of the exchange. Share your concerns with the employee and get feedback. Describe areas that need improvement. Make the exchange non-personal and nonthreatening. Aim to fix problems, not to fix blame.

Salvage Operations: Can the Marriage Be Saved?

The employee's responses should give you a feel as to whether the employee and his performance will improve. That which gets measured gets improved. After your meeting, is there a discernible improvement in performance? Check. Follow up. Does the employee sulk or work to improve the areas of concern? Is it temporary or long-term?

Be Decisive

If you become convinced that the marriage cannot be saved, resolve to pull the plug and address the situation. Be prepared to terminate. You are doing yourself and the employee no favors by prolonging the situation. If you avoid the unpleasantness, you harm the company by tolerating subpar performance. Your other reports may lose respect for you. You aren't being a humanitarian by tolerating a poor-performing employee.

Be Kind

Although it seems to be a corporate ritual, avoid terminating on a Friday. Don't get emotional, but don't be surprised if the terminated person shows emotion. Decide whether the termination will be immediate or whether you can let him work until a set future date. Discuss and provide severance pay. Decide in advance about job responsibilities like access to computer data and settlement or check authority for the period before he leaves the company.

Document

Even in so-called employment-at-will states, it is a good idea to document each poor performance episode. This may help if the employee or ex-employee later decides to file a claim for wrongful termination or discrimination. It is always difficult to terminate for poor performance when the personnel file is replete with glowing performance reviews. Alas, this is not an infrequent situation.

Part with Class

Take the high road. Unless strong reasons exist, avoid having security personnel escort people off the premises. Carefully word what you communicate to coworkers and the rest of your staff. Decide what you will tell clients and outside service vendors who worked with the departed/departing adjuster. Wish the departing adjuster well. (Be careful, though, about writing or offering to write a letter of recommendation.)

Coordinate with Human Resources

Take no action without first speaking with the Personnel or Human Resources department. Does your company have a mandatory progressive discipline process? Is the Human Resources Department in accord with what you want to do?

Distinguish between those areas in which performance is subpar and instances of dishonesty or impropriety. Know your own company's policy as to offenses that merit immediate termination. Any shenanigans regarding handling of money or property; accepting kickbacks or bribes from claimants, insureds, or vendors; acts of violence; threats of violence; and defiance or blatant insubordination may merit the most decisive termination action.

Get advance agreement from the boss and/or the Human Resources Department when you decide to fire someone so that you will not be second-guessed from above about what you did or how you did it.

Sample Notice to Company about Departing Employee

Dear Associates,

I wanted to keep you in the loop and let you know, in case you didn't already, that [insert name] has left (or will be leaving) our employ, effective [insert date]. We wish him/her luck in new pursuits.

Continuity of claims handling is very important. Therefore, we will be formulating plans for addressing his/her caseload and will be meeting further to discuss those decisions with you. In the meantime, we ask your assistance in keeping current and on top of our claim servicing obligations. We are also immediately starting a recruitment process to find a qualified replacement. (If you know of anyone who is looking for a new opportunity, please let us know!) We will keep you apprised closely of progress and efforts in this regard.

We may also look into hiring a temp adjuster as an interim measure while we pursue a recruitment process.

Please let me know if you have any questions or want to discuss these changes. Thank you in advance for helping out during this upcoming transition period.

Best regards,

Claim Supervisor or Manager

Sample Notice to Clients and Service Vendors of Staffing Change

Dear Client/Counsel/etc.

Just a note to let you know that [insert name] has left our employ, effective [insert date]. We wish him/her luck. The cases previously handled by [insert name] will—at least for the time being—be handled by [insert name]. Her phone number is _____ and her email address is _____. Continuity if claim service is very important to us. Please let me know if you have any questions or wish to discuss these changes.

Sincerely,

Claim Manager or Supervisor

Conduct an Exit Interview

Always conduct an exit interview with the departing employee. Have someone other than the supervisor conduct the exchange. Sit and listen—do not debate. You may get some valuable feedback. You may give the employee a forum for venting steam, in which case he may be less likely to file some kind of employment claim. Or, comments made in an exit interview may give a tip-off on whether you are likely to face a wrongful discharge or discrimination claim. Better to have advance notice of this so you can prepare to defend it.

Nancy Germond, President of The Insurance Writer, an agency in Jefferson City, Missouri, says,

The worst management mistake seen over and over again is that most managers want to be liked and hate to be the bad guy. You must ascertain if it's a problem that can be trained out of the person or a personality quirk. Some people think they know it all and just can't be taught anything. The excuse is, "I screwed up," and they do it over and over again. In some cases, it's the four Es of loss control (engineer out, etc.). One of them is "eliminate."

Smart Hiring Resources to Upgrade Your Claims Operation!!

None of the following books are specifically about claim department hiring, but each contains nuggets of wisdom that will help pick the right claims person for the job. Read one (or more) of these before you have to go to market and start hiring!

Topgrading: How Leading Companies Win by Hiring, Coaching and Keeping the Best People by Bradford D. Smart (Prentice Hall Press 1999)

High Impact Hiring: How to Interview and Select Outstanding Employees by Del J. Still (Management Development Systems LLC 2001)

96 Great Interview Questions to Ask Before You Hire by Paul Falcone (AMACOM 1997)

Hire With Your Head: Using POWER Hiring to Build Great Teams, 2nd Edition, by Lou Adler (John Wiley & Sons 2002)

Hiring the Best: A Manager's Guide to Effective Interviewing by Martin Yate (Adams Media Corporation 1997)

How to Compete in the War for Talent: A Guide to Hiring the Best by Carol A. Hacker (InSync Press 2001)

45 Effective Ways for Hiring Smart! How to Predict Winners and Losers in the Incredibly Expensive People-Reading Game by Pierre Mornell (Ten Speed Press 2003)

The Manager's Book of Questions: 751 Great Interview Questions for Hiring the Best Person by John Kador (AMACOM 2002)

101 Hiring Mistakes Employers Make ... And How to Avoid Them by Richard Fein (Impact Publications 2000)

If new hires are not working out, you do neither them nor the company any favors by keeping them on. If performance is sub par, you do not benefit the company by keeping them out of a warped sense of sympathy or charity. Some supervisors do not want to purge personnel deadwood. Various reasons for this exist.

Some find it unpleasant and awkward to terminate employees. Firing people is no fun. As a result, it is tempting to procrastinate and avoid such personnel problems.

The supervisor may feel sympathy with the lemon employee, knowing that cutting her loose means no paycheck. In today's economy (or in any, perhaps), that can be a devastating blow to deliver. Perhaps the supervisor or manager has not yet given up on the employee, thinking that she can rehab herself or be rehabbed.

Maybe the supervisor thinks, "A bird in the hand equals two in the bush." He knows that the replacement processmay be tedious and arduous, not to mention lengthy.

The replacement process takes lots of time, especially if done right. Here are the highlights of what claim supervisors have to do to replace an adjuster:

- Compose or update a job description.

- Compose or update a job ad.

- Wait for job ads to be placed in the newspaper and/or on the Internet.

- Prod the Human Resource or Personnel department to get going in seeking a replacement.

- Cull through resumes and phone calls. Some resumes are from people obviously unqualified for the position, so many may have to be eliminated.

- Narrow the field to promising resumes.

- Contact job candidates to schedule interviews.

- Conduct job interviews.

- Narrow the field to the most promising interviewees.

- Have short-list candidates speak with prospective coworkers, another scheduling challenge.

- Negotiate with the preferred candidate, make an offer, and agree on a start date.

- Complete all administrative and payroll paperwork needed for a new hire.

- Order new supplies to prep the new employee's work space.

- Prepare a training and/or orientation phase for the new employee.

- Reassign claims from the previous adjuster to the new one.

All of these tasks go on top of the usual day-to-day duties of a claim supervisor or manager.

An employee replacement process need not encompass all these steps, but if done right and thoroughly, it may encompass all of them and perhaps a few more. The training and orientation program is also time consuming. The higher up the replacement slot is in the organizational hierarchy, the longer this process will take.

The claim supervisor or manager must do this while juggling a myriad of other responsibilities, none of which take a break or go on holiday just because there is a personnel transition occurring.

So, sometimes supervisors may delude themselves into thinking that a poor employee is better than no employee. Or perhaps corporate has a policy—stated or not—that employees lost through attrition will not be replaced. Knowing this, the supervisor figures a poor employee is at least a warm body. Having this subpar employee may be seen as better than the supervisor himself having to take over the caseload or distributing the caseload to the remaining adjusters.

The latter can cause more problems, however, since the good employees' morale plummets. They feel used and abused. They may start looking for other jobs and quit. The problem snowballs and is exacerbated. Now the claim supervisor has a bigger problem. Instead of replacing one person, she may have to replace two or more disaffected persons who seek greener pastures.

Again, ask yourself, "Can this marriage be saved?" Can the subpar producer be trained, coached, or mentored to bring performance up to acceptable levels? Along these lines, ask yourself . . .

- Are you giving the employee clear direction?

- Does he have a clear understanding of what he has to do with regard to each claim file?

- Have you made expectations crystal clear?

- Have you given the adjuster the tools to do the job?

Other Reasons for Poor Performance

One claim manager had an employee who was a hot button with the head of the office. For some reason, the claim manager's CEO got the notion that the employee was deadwood. Nothing could dislodge this view. The CEO had picked a personal friend to head up the company's computer systems. The claim manager's report was plagued with constant computer issues. Often, for instance, she would be on a business trip and return to the office to find her computer keyboard gone, borrowed by the IT manager to use on another machine. She would return to find her password changed during a system upgrade with no prior notice to her.

As a result, she had difficulty accessing her own computer files and had to chase down the IT manager to reset the password. Her computer would spontaneously reboot, causing her to lose unsaved work. The claims manager brought these to the CEO's attention, to no avail. His buddy was the IT manager. Eventually, the employee left, the CEO felt vindicated and relieved, but the organization failed to provide the worker with the needed tools to accomplish the mission. The claims manager failed to lobby sufficiently to correct the situation.

Caseloads are another area for focus when trying to diagnose subpar performance. The best adjuster cannot do a good job if she is so overwhelmed by caseload that she is reduced to firefighting. She is in such a reactive mode that she cannot devote time to the extras that make the difference between a superficial investigation (and claim decision) and a well-grounded one. Take an average or marginal adjuster and load on 200 or 300 claim files, and you have a recipe for disaster. No wonder performance degrades. Some risk management experts believe that an optimal caseload for meaty insurance claims is between 90 and 100 per adjuster. How does your staff stack up against that number? If it compares unfavorably, maybe that is the root cause of degraded performance.

Ask yourself, "Could the adjuster do a better job—an acceptable job—with a more modest caseload?" Are you certain that the problem lies with the adjuster and not with management's workload expectations? Can you siphon off cases to see if the adjuster performs better with a more manageable load?

Keep Job Descriptions Current

Review, update, and tweak them periodically just in case one of your staff leaves. Don't wait for someone to quit before you do this. Having job descriptions current and ready to go saves time when you need to go back into the job hiring market to rapidly recruit for a replacement.

Similarly, in addition to job descriptions, keep job ads current, even if your entire staff seems extremely happy and content. Make this a diary item every six months or so. In case someone bolts, you lose no time in launching a recruitment and replacement process.

Let's close this discussion with a preventive checklist to make sure that you don't hire a lemon adjuster in the first place:

Lemon Avoidance: Adjuster Hiring Checklist

1. Invest thoroughly in the hiring process.
2. Have multiple people interview the candidate. Compare notes and impressions.
3. Check references.
4. Ask the right questions in job interviews.
5. Ask for work and writing samples.
6. Consider psychological testing using an outside professional service.
7. Communicate expectations clearly.
8. Hire for attitude—train for skills
9. Upgrade your orientation and training process to start new hires out on the right foot.

CHAPTER 8

The Uncooperative and Turncoat Insured

Your insured fails to cooperate, turns on you, demands you settle for policy limits, or else....

Most insureds are cooperative, fortunately. Occasionally, though, adjusters encounter policyholders who just seem not to care or whose whims change on the fickle winds of fate or self-interest. Or they are too busy or preoccupied to help you out.

What should the adjuster do when encountering a lack of cooperation from the insured? Here are ten steps that involve graduated responses. Let's start with the mildest response and work our way up to the hard-ball options.

First Try Diplomacy

Explain to the insured why you need her cooperation. Simply put—the insurance policy requires it. It is necessary to defend the claim or to prove the loss. It helps keep insurance premiums down. It's needed in order to process the claim.

Adjusters often assume that insureds understand all this, but many may not give it a second thought. All they know is that they have insurance and they expect you to handle the claim. Now would you please just go and do your job and leave me alone? The claims rep needs to explain that handling a claim isn't a turnkey operation. Successful claim handling is a partnership that involves a policyholder's time, effort, and commitment.

Be Persistent

Don't give up just because an insured is inaccessible or irascible. In fact, if you later disclaim coverage on grounds of no cooperation, it helps to show that you were dogged in trying to get the insured to cooperate. You can't call or phone once, then write off the situation in the face of no response. Keep plugging away, calling the insured, writing to the policyholder, asking for assistance in investigating the claim, locating witnesses, and making yourself available. In claims we've always heard that, "The squeaky wheel gets the grease." Now's the time for the adjuster to be the squeaky wheel. Be diplomatic, but be persistent, patiently explaining the need for the insured's cooperation and the fact that the insurance contract requires it.

Document Everything

Keep detailed notes, especially for every call you made or contact attempted with the insured. Copies of faxes or letters to the insured requesting cooperation should be in the file. These are self-evident tangibles that comprise a paper trail and provide documentation. If you've sent an email to the policyholder asking for help in separating damaged from undamaged property, keep a hard copy. Make sure that the adjuster notes or claim progress sheets have notations showing when and how the claims representative sought the insured's cooperation. If the insured tells the adjuster that the former is too busy to assist or won't cooperate, write that down in the claim file notes.

Approach documentation as nurses and doctors do in medical settings. There is a precept in medical malpractice litigation that, "If it's not documented in the chart, it didn't happen."

Through these actions, create a paper trail. If the insured tells you he is too busy to help, reflect that in a confirming letter. In your correspondence, itemize all attempts made to get the insured's cooperation. Refer to specific discussions and phone conversations. If you later try to disclaim coverage on grounds of noncooperation—always an uphill battle—have as much tangible evidence as possible.

Documentation may consist of letters and notes to the insured reminding him of the policy's cooperation clause, the need to help, and exactly how the insurer's ability to handle a claim is harmed by lack of cooperation. This is key, since courts usually interpret ambiguous policy language in the policyholder's favor. With regard to slights to insurers, courts tend to reason no harm, no foul. Showing how the insurer has been harmed or would be harmed by the policyholder's intransigence may help when disclaiming coverage. Prepare to show specifically how investigating or defending the case is rendered more difficult by the insured's lack of cooperation.

Involve the Agent or Broker

Explain the problem you're having. Get her on your side. Ask if she can intercede and explain the facts to the uncooperative insured. Policyholders often will listen to their insurance agents or brokers while turning deaf ears to adjusters. They don't know the adjusters but have a relationship with their agents or brokers. Further, they don't expect to have any ongoing relationship with claims representatives, which makes it easier to brush them off.

Do not wait for the insured to tell the agent her side of the story. Be proactive. Get to the agent first. See if the agent can explain how it is in everyone's interest for the policyholder to be a team player and how a lack of cooperation could negatively impact the price of her insurance or the availability of coverage.

Be realistic, though. The insurance broker represents the insurance buyer, the insured/policyholder. In most disputes, expect brokers to take their insureds' side. That's fine—they are doing their jobs. Still, it never hurts to get to them first to weigh in and explain some fundamental facts of (insurance) life to a reluctant, clamorous, or preoccupied insured.

Alert Underwriting

Adjusters can often talk till they are blue in the face, but they cannot sway a recalcitrant insured. Want a two-by-four? Enlist the underwriting department's help. Identify the underwriter on the account. Alert underwriting of any insureds with attitude or cooperation problems. Good risks have clean loss records and cooperate. Smelly risks have high loss ratios or are uncooperative.

Underwriting might be able to get an insured's attention by describing the prospect of higher insurance prices or even nonrenewal. This may get the insured's attention while the adjuster may fall short with comparable efforts. Explain to the underwriter the problem the hard-working claim folks are facing. Ask them to back you up with heavier artillery.

Quote Policy Language

Read from the word according to ISO: the Conditions section of the policy. Most policies contain language to the effect that the insured must cooperate with the insurer in investigating, defending, or settling a claim. Here is sample language from a Products and Completed Operations policy:

SECTION IV — CONDITIONS

2. Duties in The Event of Occurrence, Claim or Suit

    c. You and any other involved insured must:

        * * *

        (2) Authorize us to obtain records and other information;

        (3) Cooperate with us in the investigation, settlement or defense of the claims or suit;

Many (perhaps most?) people do *not* read their insurance policies. They find this a stupefying and dull pastime, right up there on the fun scale with reading Federal Reserve Board meeting transcripts. An insured may think that coverage is a turnkey operation: you pay your money, file the insurance policy away, and then forget about it. Why do I need to spend so much time on this claim? Isn't this what the insurance adjuster is supposed to be doing?

This is usually what in fact happens . . . unless you have a loss or an accident. Some policyholders may not realize that the policy requires them to cooperate with the claims representative. Pointing this out may soften resistance and get you the needed assistance.

Reserve Coverage Rights

Being diplomatic and nice may not work. If you have exhausted other options, consider unveiling the heavy artillery. Draft and send the insured a reservation of rights letter, quoting the cooperation clause of the insurance policy. Itemize the insured's uncooperative behavior. The letter also should state that failure to cooperate with the claim process could jeopardize the policyholder's insurance coverage. You are not quite to the point of disclaiming coverage, but you are sending a signal to the insured that you may be headed down that path.

Engage Coverage Counsel

Do you have a genuine case of no cooperation, or are you merely annoyed because an insured will not return a phone call? Have the insured's actions been so egregious that they constitute a failure to cooperate? Further, has the lack of cooperation materially hampered your investigation or handling of the claim? What is the relevant state law on abrogating coverage due to a lack of cooperation?

Even some of the best adjusters are at the deep end of the expertise pool on these types of questions. As a result, they may need the help of seasoned coverage attorneys. There is no shame in this; better safe than sorry. If you think you have a strong case for proving a lack of cooperation, ship the file to your favorite coverage attorney. Seek an advisory opinion on the odds of your prevailing.

File a Declaratory Judgment Action

Assume you have taken the preceding step and your coverage counsel agrees that (a) there has been no cooperation, (b) you can prove it, and (c) it has materially hampered your handling of the claim. You may wish to consider having coverage counsel file a declaratory judgment (often referred to as a *d.j.* or *dec* action) with the appropriate court, seeking judicial exoneration of the insurer's duties. This is the equivalent of firing the heavy artillery. You now send a strong signal to the insured that the refusal to play ball has jeopardized its insurance coverage. It may also forestall the risk of having to go to trial on the underlying claim with one hand tied behind your back due to the insured's failure to cooperate.

Dealing with an uncooperative insured is never easy. Use these tips to improve your odds of success. Even if you cross the cooperation hurdle, though, you may find another challenge looming ahead. We now turn our attention to that issue.

The Turncoat Insured

Your insured—indignant over getting sued—urged you to defend the liability claim to the bitter end, to the Supreme Court if need be. Defeat this bogus claim!!

So have you done. The case has some settlement value—you concede that and have never taken a no pay stance. Still, you feel that the claim has nowhere near the potential for policy limits or the amount of the plaintiff demand. Trial approaches. Two weeks before trial, the plaintiff attorney demands policy limits.

Seven days before trial, you get a letter from your insured or a lawyer he retained—now demanding that you settle for policy limits . . . or else. You've already spent tens of thousands of dollars in legal fees and experts preparing for trial, all with the insured's knowledge and buy in. The demand to settle is a big change in tune from the same insured that previously urged you to defend, defend, defend. You feel like you're being extorted.

What will you do?

A tough situation arises when the insured demands that you settle a claim within the policy limits . . . or else. This may be referred to as a *hammer* letter. The "or else" is typically a veiled threat of a bad faith claim and extra-contractual liability for failure to settle. Perhaps it involves a claim that has settlement value—maybe substantial settlement value—but not policy limits value. Few insureds start out insisting that the insurer pay money on a liability claim, much less policy limits. Usually, this stance develops late in the case's lifespan.

Sample Response to Hammer Letter from the Insured or the Insured's Attorney

Re:

Dear:

Thank you for your letter of [insert date] and your request that we settle the above referenced case for an amount up to your [your client's] policy limit.

As you know, we have diligently and thoroughly investigated and evaluated this case. Based on the information currently possessed—including the information provided by you/your client's defense attorney—we do not understand why you believe that [your/your client's] company's misconduct proximately caused the injury to the plaintiff to an extent that would warrant payment up to your policy limit.

This is especially mystifying since you have worked with us for quite some time in fashioning a vigorous defense to this claim. Your latest demand appears to be a significant about-face and a 180-degree turn from the prodefense strategy you had helped us formulate. Relying on that joint strategy, we have invested significant time and money in the defense of your company. Most companies have an interest in defending their company's good name and resisting claims with excessive demands.

We recognize, of course, that there may be facts you possess of which we are currently unaware.

Perhaps we misunderstand facts that are indeed known to us. Thus, please provide us with a letter detailing the misconduct you believe your company is liable for in this case, summarizing the facts indicating that such misconduct, if it occurred, proximately caused the plaintiff's claimed injuries, and summarizing why you believe that the alleged injuries have the type of value assigned to them by plaintiff's counsel. Please itemize for us as soon as possible the reasons you feel your company is legally liable to the tune of [insert amount] million.

We assure you that we will continue to make every effort to fully and fairly evaluate this case for settlement purposes. We are very concerned about our insured's interests. However, with the facts of this case as currently known, we do not see how paying or overpaying an exorbitant claim that appears to be unwarranted furthers the insured's interests. If we do that—without compelling evidence that the company really did something wrong to cause the claimed injuries to the plaintiff—you and your insurer would only be damaging yourself and other insureds by encouraging additional lawsuits of this type. Overpaying this claim might incentivize additional lawsuits and exorbitant demands that are not in your best interest.

In light of potential viable defenses to the claim, simply paying [insert amount] appears to be premature, a questionable judgment, or unwarranted. As you know, yours is not a *no fault* policy. Payments are made only in the case of proven legal liability. Further, in claims-handling practice, claim payments should bear a reasonable relationship to proven damages for which you are legally liable.

Of course, we recognize that anything can happen when a case goes to trial. Juries are notoriously unpredictable. No one can guarantee a defense verdict, and no one can rule out a sizable award. We are not dealing here in a realm of scientific certainty. Despite best efforts, unjustified results and surprises may occur. Guessing wrong—especially when done pursuant to the reasoned advice of defense counsel—is not tantamount to doing anything wrong.

However, we believe in the jury system and the ability of the citizens in [insert jurisdiction] to fairly and justly evaluate the evidence in this case to reach a verdict based not upon emotions—but upon the facts and law.

Put differently, it has not been established that there is a probability of an excess verdict. Relying on defense counsel's advice, we believe there is—with a vigorous defense—a potential likelihood of a defense verdict or an award less than the plaintiff's exorbitant demand.

We look forward to receiving your response as soon as possible [or within ____ days] so that we can reassess our position regarding the plaintiff's demand in light of the information you provide us.

Sincerely,

Your options in such situations often boil down to (1) doing nothing, (2) making an offer higher than your last but below policy limits, or (3) offering policy limits. Some alternatives for this type of situation follow.

Renegotiate Any and All Deadlines

Buy yourself some time to weigh your options and decide what to do. The problem that often arises, however, is that insureds make such demands very close to the date of a trial or settlement conference.

Meet with Coverage Counsel

Ask her to review the file quickly but thoroughly. What does she recommend? Do you have any alternative to caving in to the policy limits demand? What does the law say in that jurisdiction about insured demands to pay policy limits? Can you rely on the assessment of defense counsel? Does the law presume bad faith if you guess wrong?

Ask for Details

Press the insured's representative to explain the reasons for the demand to pay policy limits. Liability policies are, by definition, contracts that only pay in the event of legal liability. They are not *no fault* policies. They do not constitute a line of credit for an insured to draw upon in order to avoid having to deal with a troublesome lawsuit. Typically for a policy limits settlement to occur there must be a combination of clear legal liability on the insured's part plus severe damages to the plaintiff. It is always awkward for the insured to explain why it feels legally liable; even more so if an insured has spent months (maybe years) telling the adjuster that the claim was bogus, frivolous, without merit, or exaggerated. Why the change of heart so suddenly? Please help us understand.

Usually, the insured's demand letter will not offer a rationale. It may not itemize the reasons why the insured is legally liable or why the damages are catastrophic. Press for details. It's too bad that you have been led down the path of defense, only to have your insured, which goaded you down this path, start erecting roadblocks and threatening you if you don't change course.

Many insureds will be less able to articulate the reasons for its legal liability, yet that is a precondition for paying under a legal liability policy.

Respond to All Demands

Even if all you do is thank the insured for the letter, make sure you are prompt in acknowledging each one. Advise the insured that you will certainly consider the matter. Never give the insured the ammo to say, "Not only did they fail to settle the case, but they were lax in responding to correspondence!"

Alert Underwriting

Many times in this situation you are faced with having to pay a premium on a settlement—in effect to overpay a settlement—because an insured made a (poor) business judgment to buy low limits, to not purchase sufficient insurance. Rather than take the consequences for that business decision, it is easier to make the adjuster and his policy limits the fall guys to get rid of a troublesome claim. Sometimes these situations occur because an insured opted not to buy much insurance coverage. Other times the situation exists because the insured was not able to purchase any more coverage, or because the excess market capacity was very tight. (This has often been the case in hard-to-place lines of coverage such as nursing homes.)

There is often a connection and correlation between having low limits and demanding that the insurer pay policy limits. The prospect of an uninsured excess verdict increases the lower the limits carried by a policyholder. To avoid the risk, such an under-insured entity is a prime candidate for hammering the insurer with a demand that it settle or else.

The insured's coercing you to overpay a claim for whatever reason is something to report to the account underwriter. Explain the situation to her. This may be a factor that the underwriter will want to weigh in renewal and pricing decisions.

Settle!

Not to overlook the obvious, consider settling the case. Maybe you are better off paying policy limits than rolling the dice. If you pay or offer the policy limits, then the most you can pay is, well, the policy limits.

If you roll the dice and guess wrong, a jury may come back with an award exceeding policy limits. Then, the insured may sue you. In that case, the most you can pay is, well, policy limits plus. In effect, there may not be a cap on your company's ultimate potential liability. Plus, you now must pay extra defense costs and take the case through to trial. Plus, you get to deal with your company's E&O insurer. Plus, you get to spend hours on a two-front war:

1. defending the underlying case and its possible appeal

2. defending the excess liability claim for the insured

Which risk is greater?

The point is not to automatically roll over and play dead whenever an insured says, "Pay up." But also do not get drawn into a test of wills with the insured or her privately retained counsel. Do not invest your ego or get your back up in order to prove, "No one is going to tell *me* what to do!" Step back and assess the situation objectively. Weigh the relative merits. Do not rule out the possibility that settlement does indeed make sense.

Demands in Excess of Policy Limits

Do you have a demand within policy limits? You get a letter from the insured's personal attorney, demanding that you settle the claim within policy limits. There's one small problem, though. The demand is $7.5 million. Your policy limit is $5 million. Consider replying that you are trying to settle the case but the insured must understand that the current demand is for more than policy limits.

One Practitioner's Perspective

Lyle Walker, President of Walker Risk Management, Allen Park, MI says

An insured doesn't "just get cold feet." Something, somebody, or someone's previous actions cause this to happen. It could even be this insured just got a premium increase because of past loss activity and for the first time starts looking at losses. Rarely is it just a single claim that causes an insured to get active in the adjustment of the claim, but rather any number of things can activate such interest.

Nothing in any policy says how the insurance carrier will handle the claim. The policy describes what is and what isn't covered and that the carrier will defend the insured. Most insureds do not know this or at least are not willing to accept it. Nor does the carrier have a duty to tell the insured about counsel selected. Anyway, we have a claim department handling a claim requesting the insured's cooperation but not accepting their advice or desires on how the claim should be handled.

So we reach the point where the insured is taking an active interest in the handling of the claim and inserting himself into the process with all kinds of advise and directions to the carrier, which is essentially ignoring them. Each has the other in the cross hairs of their weapons.

The only way to handle or smooth the waters is to get the players involved in a face-to-face discussion on neutral ground. The carrier must be prepared to explain its actions to date and how it intends to proceed. The insured must be prepared to state whatever it is that is its problem. Quiet discussion with full disclosure has and usually will at least quiet things down. Usually the insured's reasons for being anxious about the handling will come out. Such exposure is usually not comfortable for the insured and it backs away. Often, pertinent information about the claim comes forth as a result of the discussion and is acted upon. If done gently, the insured becomes aware of what position it has contractually and will back away. The carrier can and should show great respect for whatever is really bothering the insured and even suggest actions the insured can take to build a defense or prevent such claims from happening in the first place. Carefully.

Talking things out will solve most problems 85 percent of the time.

Faint-Hearted Insureds

By Donald C. Erickson, Partner

Murtaugh, Miller, Meyer, & Nelson LLP
Irvine, California

Question:

The insured—indignant over getting sued—urged you to defend to the death. Defeat this bogus claim!! So have you done. The case has some settlement value, but nowhere near the policy limits on the level of the plaintiff demand. Trial date approaches. The plaintiff attorney has demanded policy limits. You just got a letter from your insured, or a lawyer he retained—demanding now that you settle for your policy limits . . . or else.

That's a big change in tune, this from the sane insured who previously urged you to defend, defend, defend. You feel like you're being extorted.

Any analysis of this question takes place against the omnipresent backdrop of the general rule that an insurer that rejects a demand by the insured to settle within the policy limits has "uncapped" its policy limits and is liable for any excess verdict that may be returned. [*Certain Underwriters of Lloyd's v. General Accident Ins. Co.*, 909 F.2d 228 (7th Cir. 1990); *Steele v. Hartford Fire Ins. Co.*, 788 F.2d 441 (7th Cir. 1986).] Understandably, sophisticated insureds have implemented policies in claims negotiation that require the legal division or risk manager to demand the acceptance of any offer within the limits or efforts to settle at the limits in every case. The demand on the carrier costs nothing and secures the insured additional "free insurance" for the amount of any excess award.

Demand Within Limits

In most jurisdictions, no formal demand from the insured on the carrier is required—it is enough that the carrier rejected a demand from the claimant within the limits when an excess verdict was likely. As stated in *City of Hobbs v. Hartford Fire Ins. Co.*, 162 F.3d 576 (10th Cir. 1998) "We conclude that when there is a **substantial likelihood of recovery in excess of limits**, an insurer's unwarranted refusal to settle is a breach of the implied covenant of good faith and fair dealing." In that case, the court held that the prerequisite to the later bad faith claim is the opportunity to settle within the limits (the court interpreted an offer by claimant's counsel to recommend $600,000 as an "opportunity to settle").

Some courts have gone further and expanded the carrier's obligation to include initiating or **seeking out** settlement opportunities. [*Maine Bonding & Cas. Co. v. Centennial Ins. Co.*, 693 P.2d 1296 (Or. 1985) (under Oregon law, insurer's duty "may require that an insurer make inquiries to determine if settlement is possible within the policy limitations."); *Rova Farms Resort, Inc. v. Investors Ins. Co. of America,* 323 A.2d 495 (N.J. 1974) (insurer, having restricted negotiating power of insured, had positive fiduciary duty to take the initiative and attempt to negotiate a settlement within the policy coverage); *State Auto Ins. Co. v. Rowland,* 427 S.W.2d 30 (Tenn. 1968) ("to hold as a matter of law that an [insurer] cannot be guilty of bad faith unless it received an offer . . . within the policy limits could most certainly lead to inequitable results."); *Fulton v. Woodford,* 545 P.2d 979 (Ariz. Ct. App. 1976); *Alt v. American Family Mut. Ins. Co.,* 237 N.W.2d 706 (Wis. 1976); *Hartford Ins. Co. v. Methodist Hospital,* 785 F. Supp. 38 (E.D.N.Y. 1992).]

Other courts do not appear to require the same effort on the part of the carrier. [*Commercial Union Ins. Co. v. Mission Ins. Co.,* 835 F.2d 587 (5th Cir. 1988) (Louisiana law—no obligation to make a "pre-emptive offer" of the policy limits in response to demands in excess of the limits); *Ranger Ins. Co. v. Home Indem. Co.,* 741 F. Supp. 716 (N.D. Ill. 1990) ("suggestions" by unauthorized negotiator were not a "firm offer to settle within the limits"); *American Physicians Ins. Exchange v. Garcia,* 876 S.W.2d 842 (Tex. 1994) ("a *Stowers* settlement demand must propose to release the insured fully in exchange for a stated sum of money").] In *Delancy v. St. Paul Fire & Marine Ins. Co.,* 947 F.2d 1536 (1991), the 11th Circuit, applying Georgia law, held that the insured has the burden of proving that the carrier actually knew or should have known that the claim could be settled within the policy limits.

It would appear to be in the best interests of the carrier to elicit a written demand from claimant's counsel whenever the value of the case approaches or exceeds the policy limits. In addition to making a record of the super-limits demands of the claimant, an ongoing written dialogue may encourage the claimant to assess the real strengths and weaknesses of her case.

Unreasonable Rejection

Some courts have imposed a second requirement that the carrier has acted unreasonably in rejecting the demand within limits. In *American Physicians,* the court articulated the Texas (*Stowers* doctrine) rule as follows:

"The *Stowers* duty is not activated by a settlement demand unless three prerequisites are met: (1) the claim against the insured is within the scope of coverage, (2) the demand is within the policy limits, and (3) the terms of the demand are such that an ordinarily prudent insurer would accept it, considering the likelihood and degree of the insured's potential exposure to an excess judgment."

It is frequently said that the duty to settle arises whenever (1) the carrier is in receipt of an offer within the limits (see above) and (2) there is a "substantial likelihood of a recovery in excess of the policy limits."

Reverse or Comparative Bad Faith

Some decisions have alluded to a possible reciprocal duty of good faith and fair dealing running from the insured to the insurer—a violation of which results in so-called "reverse bad faith" and is asserted as an offset to the liability of the carrier for "bad-faith" failure to settle. As articulated in *California Casualty Gen. Ins. Co. v. Superior Court*, 218 Cal. Rptr. 817 (Cal. Ct. App. 1985), the doctrine was an extension of the general rule of comparative tort liability: that whenever two tortfeasors have combined to inflict an injury, fairness requires that liability be apportioned between them according to their fault. Unfortunately, the doctrine has not been adopted in any other jurisdiction of which I am aware, and the *California Casualty* case was disapproved by the California Supreme Court in *Kransco v. American Empire Surplus Lines Ins. Co.*, 97 Cal. Rptr. 2d 151 (2000). The court explained that the quasi-fiduciary duty of good faith and fair dealing owed by the parties to an insurance contract is a one-way street—it is owed by the carrier to the insured, not by the insured to the carrier.

The court pointed out, however, that the carrier is not without remedies where the insured has behaved badly: the insured's conduct may render the carrier's own conduct more reasonable, and hence less actionable [*Blake v. Aetna Life Ins. Co.*, 160 Cal. Rptr. 528 (Cal. Ct. App. 1979)] or the insured's misconduct may breach the policy cooperation clause [*Campbell v. Allstate Ins. Co.*, 32 Cal. Rptr. 827, (Cal. 1963)], which is regarded as a condition to coverage in many jurisdictions.

Rights of/Duties to Excess Carriers

In some jurisdictions, the liability of a nonsettling primary carrier does not extend to excess carriers required to pay on the judgment. In such jurisdictions, the limits are not uncapped as to an excess carrier because (a) the primary carrier is not in privity with the excess carrier, and (b) owes no direct duty in tort to the excess carrier. See *Puritan Ins. Co. v. Canadian Universal Ins. Co.*, 775 F.2d 76 (3d Cir. 1985) [also, no bad faith because insured approved the decision to try the case, with full information]. See also: *McNally v. Nationwide Ins. Co.*, 815 F.2d

254 (3d Cir. 1986); *Pacific Employers Ins. Co. v. United General Ins. Co.*, 664 F. Supp. 1022 (W.D. La. 1987).

In most sophisticated jurisdictions, the excess carrier is held to be equitably subrogated to the rights of the insured against the nonsettling primary carrier, subject to defenses the primary carrier would have against a similar claim by the insured. [*Westchester Fire Ins. Co. v. General Star Indem. Co.*, 183 F.3d 578 (7th Cir. 1999); *Twin City Fire Ins. Co. v. Country Mutual Ins. Co.*, 23 F.3d 1175 (7th Cir. 1994); *Insurance Co. of North America v. Medical Protective Co.*, 768 F.2d 315 (10th Cir. 1985); *Continental Casualty Co. v. Royal Ins. Co.*, 219 Cal. App. 3d 111 (App. Dist 1, 1990); *United States Fire Ins. Co. v. Morrison Assurance Co.*, 600 So. 2d 1147 (Fla. Dist. Ct. App. 1992).]

In a minority of states, the primary carrier is said to owe a direct duty to the excess carrier, and questions of subrogation are immaterial. [*Ranger Ins. Co. v. Home Indem. Co.*, 714 F. Supp. 956 (N.D. Ill. 1989); *Vencill v. Continental Casualty Co.*, 433 F. Supp. 1371 (S.D.W.Va. 1977); *Zurich Ins. Co. v. State Farm Mutual Auto. Ins. Co.*, 524 N.Y.S.2d 202 (N.Y. App. Div. 1988); *Commercial Union Ins. Co. v. Medical Protective Co.*, 393 N.W.2d 479 (Mich. 1986); *Western World Ins. Co. v. Allstate Ins. Co.*, 376 A.2d 177 (N.J. Super. Ct. App. Div. 1977). *See also American Home Assur. Co. v. Dykema, Gossett, Spencer, Goodnow & Trigg*, 625 F. Supp. 1052 (N.D. Ill. 1985).]

In summary, the carrier whose insured has suddenly decided to settle at all costs would be well advised to:

- Immediately try to unobtrusively elicit a settlement demand from the claimant;
- Disclose the demand to and discuss it with the insured;
- Secure an opinion from defense counsel regarding case value, especially regarding whether an excess verdict is "highly probable" or "substantially likely";
- If you conclude that an excess verdict is unlikely, stick to your guns and advise the insured of your decision and the reasons therefore;
- If you conclude that an excess verdict is likely, and if the demand is in excess of remaining limits, request the insured advise in writing whether they are willing to contribute the difference.
- Whether or not you conclude that an excess verdict is likely, if the case involves a substantial likelihood of punitive damages, inquire of the insured whether it is willing to make a contribution in lieu of punitives; and
- If the insured has engaged in conduct other than demanding a settlement that is detrimental to settlement value, document the conduct in writing to the insured.

CHAPTER 9

Dealing with the Psycho-client from Hell

Fantasy versus reality

In a perfect world for adjusting firms and claim departments, clients would be calm and polite. They would be crystal-clear in communicating the nature and scope of adjusting assignments. They would pay bills on time and pose no collection problems. They would recognize a job well done and quickly point out any shortcomings in service.

So much for fantasy.

In the real world, adjusting firms and insurer claim departments find that clients run the gamut from the delightful to the distasteful. While most clients—be they insurance companies, insureds, or self-insureds—draw little negative attention to themselves, difficult clients can command a disproportionate amount of time and energy.

How do you deal with them?

The toughest of the tough clients we call the *Psycho-Clients from Hell.* The ability to spot and manage relationships with the prickliest clients can often spell the difference between success and failure for individual adjusters, adjusting firms, and claim departments. Beyond this, having a protocol for dealing with difficult clients can save adjusters much emotional wear and tear.

Psycho-clients from hell can exact a heavy toll. Though they may generate revenue, they may spawn more antacid consumption. The heartburn factors include:

- job stress from having to deal with them since they degrade the quality of one's work life

- collection and accounts receivable issues from slow payers

- low morale by those who are saddled with doing their work

- the time drain required to deal with them

- potential loss of key employees who just can't take dealing with them

- unprofitable business when servicing time is disproportionate to the fee or premium income

- legal headaches from the possibility of litigious, suit-happy customers

Oops—I just breached a sacred maxim of customer service, "The customer is always right."

Baloney!

In insurance claims, that can spell trouble real fast.

- The customer wants you to pay the claim that isn't covered. Is the customer right?

- The customer wants you to take the damages as proven without any documentation. Use the honor system. Is that right?

- The customer wants you to overpay the claim because of a business relationship or to placate a customer in a no-liability situation. Is that right?

- The customer wants you to assume the defense of a related company even though it does not qualify as an additional insured. Is that right?

- The customer wants you to accept coverage because its broker screwed up by not getting the right coverage to start with. OK with that?

- The insured wants you to disgorge your complete policy limits because it failed to buy enough insurance. No problem, right?

This is just a sampling of situations that the claims professional may face. In the short run, it is tempting to relent. Much pressure may be brought to bear on the adjuster—menacing letters, threats to pull the account, phone calls to the adjuster's boss, desperate appeals to the underwriters, and complaints to the state insurance department.

The short run temptation is to give in. Smooth the waters.

This is a recipe for short-term gain and long-term pain, though. The customer is not always right.

Caveat

Pick and choose your battles with care. Be selective in drawing a line in the sand with your clients. If you find this a daily occurrence, then something is probably wrong.

How do you extricate yourself from untenable client situations? How do you dump a bad client for reasons other than non-payment of invoices?

Let's examine some practical ways to spot and manage the psychoclient from hell.

One way to avoid such problems is by never accepting assignments from this type of client to start with. Following are a few telltale red-light danger signs.

Trigger-happy Customers

These include clients who come to you right after having fired another adjusting company. If they fired one, what makes you think that they won't be quick to pull the trigger on you as well? It's like a claims-conscious claimant, on whom the Index Bureau shows three prior claims. When you see a claimant with a claims or adjuster history, your guard should be up.

Fickle Clients

Beware too of the client with a claims history and a track record of playing musical adjusters. Some clients are quick to fall in and out of love with adjusters and adjusting companies. They should spell C-A-U-T-I-O-N for the wary independent adjuster.

The Pasha Client

This customer enjoys beauty contests and subjects incumbent vendors to periodic, ritualistic exercises. This is another red flag danger sign. They may enjoy boosting their own sense of self-importance by having new suitors parade before them. They may gratify their ego by being fawned over by new adjusting or insurance candidates. Or perhaps the client company has high turnover, which results in revolving-door vendor selection, as each new hire wants to put his or her own stamp on the claims side of the program.

Entitlement Clients

These types make it clear that they expect extras if you get the business: expecting to be wined and dined, perhaps with spouse in tow; expense account paid trips to exotic locales; and other types of favors in exchange for hiring you.

Chip-on-the-shoulder Clients

These customers are loaded for bear with regard to adjusting companies. In a prior lifetime the contact person may have been an adjuster or even an employee of your company who parted ways acrimoniously. Now is payback time for the client who has an ax to grind. You may never know what kind of psychological baggage a client carries around from her job or personal life, baggage that causes you to be the lightning rod for pent-up frustration, anger, and bad mood.

Kill-the-messenger Clients

Unfortunately, adjusters and adjusting companies are frequently in the uncomfortable role of delivering bad news: the little claim now looks serious; we need to consider settling for $100,000; our expert witness just cratered under a withering deposition; the jury returned an award for $3 million. (See Chapter 4 on *Killing the Messenger.*)

Haggler Clients

This type quibbles and nags over every single service bill. This psycho-client from hell frequently (perhaps constantly) has trouble with your service bills and seeks to cut them each month, with unwarranted write-downs and discounts. These clients may love you at first . . . until they get your invoice. Then you are in for a fight.

Abusive Clients

These clients may be short-tempered. They may blow up at the adjuster, accusing her of being incompetent, lazy, or crooked. Some clients unfortunately seem inherently abusive and think that hiring a claim service is a license to dump on the adjusters. This could include insulting them, cussing them out, or even making improper advances toward one of them.

The Foot-dragger

This client is chronically late in paying service bills. Some clients simply drag their feet in paying service bills or plead cash-flow problems.

The Charity Case

This client always wants something for nothing. Those who ask for or demand things that are beyond the original claim service agreement or contract fall within this category.

The Preoccupied Client

This individual is too busy to work with you on the case. One client I've dealt with periodically complains that we don't take enough cases to trial, that we don't get in there and flight it out with the plaintiffs. During one case of his that we took to trial, however, he balked at the time demands trial preparation demanded. The insured's CEO was aghast when defense counsel told him how much time he'd need to be available for depositions and for trial. The attitude seems to be, "Take all my cases to trial, but don't impose on my time."

A Tale from the Field

A friend works for an insurer that is saddled with a prickly commercial policyholder. The insured has a $50,000 per loss retention, but the insurer handles claims as if they were first-dollar: hiring attorneys, paying them, and then invoicing the policyholder. This insured is notorious for holding up reimbursement to the insurer as he nit-picks the attorney's bill to death or claims that "the claim shouldn't have cost so much." Although the policyholder has a decent loss ratio, the insurer was tempted to nonrenew the account. The hassle-factor and static associated with servicing the account was so severe that not even history and a good loss ratio could carry the day. Servicing some clients is a thankless task, and adjusting company management may decide that life is too short to tolerate such stress.

If a client doesn't respect your expertise and refuses to consider your recommendations, you might consider terminating the relationship even if the revenue stream is sweet. (This admittedly works better if you work for a third-party claims administrator.) You know, the claim you recommend paying that the client insists on taking to trial; the defensible case that can be won, except the insured demands that you settle it. Some clients view adjusting firms as commodities.

Dumping a troublesome client is not an elegant decision and is typically a last-ditch remedy, an end-game solution where there virtually are no winners. No one wants such a situation, especially since most independent adjusting firms these days need every client they can get.

For some adjusting companies, though, it can lead to a win-win solution. Adjusting firms get a big monkey off their backs and are free to pursue more profitable quarry. The clients also are more satisfied. Here are some tips and advice:

Spell Everything out in the Contract

One safeguard: when setting up an account, insist on a written contract. This should cover items like bills, billing frequency, rates, scope of service, and timeliness of payments. A buttoned down contract may be your best protection against difficult clients if it becomes necessary to terminate the relationship.

Consider the Claims Equivalent of a Prenuptial Agreement

In advance, establish a series of frequent checkpoints, when you and the client sit down and discuss progress and strategy. At these discussions or beforehand, ask if you can really help. The key is prevention, and the checkpoint approach works well.

Give Notice

If firing the client becomes necessary, don't burn any bridges. Relax and shed emotional baggage. The chip on your shoulder may be noticeable to new clients or prospects, so make sure that you have your head together before moving on.

Richard Ackroyd, President of Richard Ackroyd and Associates of Edmonton, Alberta, Canada, states that, "it can pay to 'dump' clients, but one question that lingers involves the ethical responsibility of the claims representative to maintain the profits of his or her employer." Some clients might be difficult in the sense of demanding more from the claim vendor than was originally negotiated, more than was called for in the contract. Other clients might be unwilling to supply the information necessary to handle a claim or fulfill a claim service contract, or they may renege on paying negotiated fees agreed upon up-front. But getting rid of those clients will cost the adjusting company some revenue.

Let Them Down Easy

Say something like, "It seems that things aren't really working out well between us. We've worked very hard, but nothing we do seems to be enough. Perhaps we should consider an amicable divorce. If you are not getting the service you deserve despite our best efforts, maybe you would be better served by looking elsewhere. What do you think?"

Or:

"If, despite our best efforts, we can't seem to meet your standards, maybe you would be better off sending your claim assignments elsewhere. We would be happy to work with any new vendor you choose to orchestrate a smooth transition when they take your files."

You might be pleasantly surprised to find that, when facing this stark option, the client mellows and insists that things aren't so bad after all. It may even inspire some positive introspection on the part of psycho-clients, prompting them to reform their obnoxious behavior. Further, you show that you can parry their ultimate trump card. No longer can they yank your chain by threatening discharge. This comment telegraphs that you have already considered it and don't necessarily view it as a negative.

Charge More

This tactic works for TPAs. (Insurers may be able to raise premiums to account for the hassle that certain clients present.) One way to perform a de facto dump is to raise rates. In effect, this is an indirect way to jettison a difficult client. Then you can always feign crocodile tears, all the while happy that you're rid of a headache-intensive customer.

Some folks might be antagonistic toward dumping any client. After all, claim services and adjusters are problem-solvers. Don't difficult clients need help too?

Perhaps, but if you become so personally involved in the client's issues that you can't be effective anymore, perhaps you should reconsider the relationship. Volunteer to make a referral or even be involved in the process of selecting the replacement.

Some adjusting firms may feel that they cannot economically afford to dump any clients. After all, the economy is tight. Competition for business is fierce. Clients are hard to find. More and more insurers and self-insureds seem to be selective about outsourcing, internalizing the claims handling function. The upshot is heightened competition, a shrinking pie fought for by the same number of adjusting services. Dumping a client can also be seen as surrender, as admitting that you couldn't do the job, or as giving in to the client's complaints.

Other adjusting firms or insurers may, however, decide that

- life is too short for the stress;

- dealing with a difficult client is demotivating to the adjusting staff;

- the psycho-client is an unprofitable account, after you factor in collection problems and the (non-billable) hours spent dealing with the client;

- a client may lead them into dubious legal terrain, such as denying claims that should be paid or slowing down payments on legitimate claims in order to accommodate the client's cash flow problems; or

- maybe the best thing to do to a competitor is to let them have the treat of trying to placate the hard-to-please client. Sweet revenge!

Shedding a difficult client should be a last resort to be undertaken only in extraordinary circumstances. In business, a common maxim is, "There are two things in life you can't choose: your parents and your clients."

Maybe true—maybe not. Use these tips and tactics to navigate through the rough waters of oddball clients and customer disaffection.

Are *you* a psycho-client from hell?

Don't be! Claim adjusters do have clients, but there is a whole spectrum of service providers for whom adjusters are either clients or customers. These include: defense attorneys, coverage attorneys, vocational rehab vendors, structured settlement firms, body shops and repair facilities, contractors, fire and smoke restoration specialists, damage estimators, rental car firms, and accident reconstruction specialists.

As claims professionals absorb abuse from others, it may be tempting to lay it back onto the folks with whom we work. To get better service, though, heed the lessons of those clients you find distasteful. Resolve not to model such behavior but to set a good example. Be courteous and professional. Pay bills on time. If you have a complaint, communicate it in a direct but not insulting way. Exhaust all options with your contact before going over his head to the boss. Make sure you have all your facts straight. Be specific in what you want done to correct the problem.

Be the kind of client toward your vendors that vendors *want* to work with. That is how you get the best service for the best price—by *not* being a psycho-client from hell.

CHAPTER *10*

With Friends like These . . .

Your defense attorney turns
out to be a lemon

You're in the middle of a trial. The stakes are high—policy limits or beyond. You've prepared your case every which way you know how. You feel pretty confident because you're going into battle with one of your strongest defense attorneys.

Or so you thought.

Your strong attorney calls you, sobbing. He says that he cannot take the pressure. His family life and peace of mind are suffering. He is very sorry and hopes you understand. Hopefully the court will let you bring in new counsel.

Have a nice day and good luck on your case!

Now, you're *the one who feels like sobbing. What will you do?*

Fox TV has the most interesting shows: *When Animals Attack, Man Versus Beast,* and *Joe Millionaire.* These dramas pale in comparison to the turmoil you feel, however, when you are deep into a serious claim and discover that your defense attorney is a lemon. The seeds of doubt may sprout as little shoots at first, but they soon take root and grow as fast as poison ivy.

Maybe the attorney was highly recommended, but things can happen to degrade an attorney's performance.

He might delegate to one or more other attorneys, perhaps associates who are not as adept as he is. Many law firms are big proponents of the team concept. There is nothing inherently wrong with this. In some cases, though, this may meet the law firm's needs more than the client's, and accountability may be lost. The partner to whom you assigned the case may rarely sign the reports that you're getting. Perhaps you do not see the desired attorney's fingerprints on the file. Maybe you weren't even consulted at all about the staffing decisions.

The attorney might undergo some personal situation during the case that undermines his performance. This could include illness, substance abuse, divorce, or tax problems.

Personal Experience

I had a trial in Allentown, Pennsylvania, in which the defense lawyer— a highly regarded attorney with a large national firm—complained about the stress he felt in trying the case. In another instance in Houston, defense counsel phoned during trial to half-jokingly suggest that he might have a nervous breakdown. Needless to say, this was not the kind of feedback I was looking for at this stage. The complaints did not fill me with confidence, and I wondered how I got myself in these positions.

Much depends on where you are in the case's life cycle, which determines the amount of leeway you have to switch attorneys. For example, if the case is less than ninety days old and you are not yet deep into it, you may be able to make a seamless transition to new defense counsel. You can tell the old counsel that you wish to make a change and then proceed to do so. You need not delve into a lot of detail.

On the other hand, perhaps you are ninety days before trial. Or you are in trial. In these cases, you will be hard pressed to change defense counsel. The costs to get a new firm up to speed on the case may be prohibitive, making successful defense even more problematic.

The insured policyholder may also be rattled by anything that looks like you are changing horses midstream. You fear the distraction of potential flak from the insured, who may be unnerved.

Further, the turmoil in the defense camp may send a signal to the opposing side that you are in disarray, a signal not conducive to fruitful settlement negotiations.

Is a Switch Necessary?

Having said that, depending on the degree of impairment exhibited by counsel, a switch may be needed. Perhaps you can transition from one attorney in the firm to another, from a weak to a strong advocate. This may be a preferred route in lieu of a wholesale change of law firm.

Ask yourself, "Can I rehab this situation? Is it a correctable problem?" When coaching adjusters about subpar attorneys, I often say, "Don't fire them—fire them up!" Get their attention. Itemize the concerns.

Is the problem one of

- basic competence?

- nonresponsiveness?

- lack of cost consciousness and sensitivity?

- poor chemistry?

Some of these are more easily corrected than others. If you sense that the lawyer is just not competent, there is likely little you can do to fix the situation. The sooner you move to a new attorney, the better.

Nonresponsiveness could mean not answering mail, email, faxes, or phone calls.

Or, it could mean answering them in a tardy or desultory fashion.

Or it could mean responding promptly but with evasive responses on one or more key issues about which you've specifically inquired. Some attorneys are adroit in getting claims people off-topic. Sometimes it's like nailing Jell-O® to the wall to get them to answer basic questions like, "What is the case worth?" or "What are our percentage odds of a defense verdict?" You may need to place a wake-up call to defense counsel, setting forth your service standards and explaining where the attorney needs to improve. This may be an effective way to fire him up.

If cost-effectiveness is a factor, put that on the table for discussion. Explain your concerns in a businesslike nonaccusatory way. Has the attorney exceeded her budget? (You are requiring budgets, aren't you?) Are there whopper bills? Do the bills look heavy on certain types of charges and entries? (Read and review can be a notorious cost sinkhole.) Are there stray charges that you do not understand? Entries of attorneys that you do not recognize?

These are all red lights on your litigation management dashboard that may signal a need for probing and corrective action. Other remedies when you see troubling signs include the following:

Schedule a Conference Call

Carve out some time so that you can address the issues in an undistracted manner. Prepare an agenda. List your concerns. Use nouns and verbs. Avoid adjectives, especially words like sloppy, incompetent, and sluggish. Be blandly descriptive. Segue from reciting problems into listing your requirements, such as:

- "We want phone calls returned within twenty-four hours."

- "We want emails answered within forty-eight hours."

- "We want responsive answers when we ask about case value."

- "We want you to talk to us before you delegate or make staffing changes on our case."

- "We want advance warning of any budget-busting bills."

Invite the Attorney to Your Office

You need to beat some attorneys over the head (figuratively) with a two-by-four to get their attention. Subtlety does not work. Emails don't work. Letters or faxes don't register. Phone calls don't put you on the same page. In situations like this, host a meeting at your office and invite the attorney to attend. Make it clear that this time and expense should be off the meter. Hopefully this will not be necessary, but you never know.

Personal War Story

I had a case with a Florida attorney. He had a six-figure case, but before negotiating a decent settlement he drove me crazy. He delegated like mad to a young associate whom I thought was in over her head. Although I had assigned the case to him specifically, few of his fingerprints were on the case. The firm routinely blew through early alert billing requirements, mandating that we get advance notice of all invoices exceeding $5,000 per quarter. ("They'll all be over $5,000," was his reply.) One interim bill exceeded $40,000.

When the associate called me for settlement authority, I asked her what she felt was a reasonable compromise settlement value for my insured. She was so flummoxed, you might have thought I asked her to explain Einstein's Theory of Relativity.

Fortunately, we settled the case. Sensing some unfinished business regarding the litigation handling process, though, I invited the firm to my office to conduct a postmortem and to set things straight. We needed to get on the same page as respects budgeting, cost forecasting, case staffing, cost management, early evaluations—the basics.

Weeks before the planned meeting, I received a bill in the mail for $1,800 for two plane tickets to my office and back. Astonished, I thought I had seen everything. I wrote to the attorney, telling him that this was not amusing, that he was certainly pushing the envelope and to please, please tell me this was a mistake. Three days later, he emailed me saying "Holy Cow!"; it was a mistake his secretary had made. (The bill even referenced a file that did not involve any of my company's policyholders!)

Attorneys hear accounts like this and guffaw that things like this do not happen. Let me tell you something as a professional client—they *do*!

Moral:

- Do not pay for time or expense to fix service problems. That should be on the lawyer's dime, not yours.
- Beware of attorneys who fail to take accountability for their mistakes and play blame the secretary for problems.

Go Visit Her

Another tactic is to arrange to visit the lawyer in question. This is more time-efficient for the lawyer, less so for you. The lawyer is less apt to be defensive, though, if you meet her on her own turf.

Before the meeting, decide whether you want to ride the same horse or look in another stable. In doing so, be thinking of Plan B. Have another firm ready to go, waiting in the wings.

Explore Other Sources of Legal Talent

Continuously build your bench strength. Here are six sources for good defense attorneys:

1. Consider word of mouth recommendations from other claims people handling the same types of claims.

2. Call an independent adjusting company office or TPA in the region where you have a need. Explain your situation. Ask for a few recommendations. Ask them to rank their recommendations. (This is why it is handy to save those office directories that you periodically get from independent adjusting companies.)

3. Ask clients for recommendations of goods firms with which they have worked. (You also earn good karma points with your client by showing that you respect their judgment and recommendation.)

4. Ask your existing network of defense attorneys. Get all their email addresses. Build a mailing list of defense attorneys. When you need a lawyer, put out an email bulletin describing your need and the geographic area. When I do this I usually get six to twelve recommendations from my existing cadre of defense lawyers within hours. This provides a pool of candidates with which to work.

5. Check the free Martindale-Hubbell (www.martindalehub bell.com) attorney directory. I would not make an attorney selection solely on the basis of Martindale-Hubbell, but it may provide insight on a lawyer's background, experience, and areas of expertise.

6. Check legal groups and directories. These include the American Law Firm Association, Federation of Corporate Counsel, Federation of Insurance Defense Counsel, The Trial Network, The Harmonie Group, and *Lex Mundi* (especially for claims outside the United States).

Take Your Staff's Temperature

Have your staff alert you to problems with defense counsel. Otherwise you may be oblivious to the quality of service being delivered because, if you're a manager, you may not be actively managing files. As a person rises through the claims and organizational hierarchy, her active caseload tends to diminish. You will likely not find the top claims people, for example, at most large insurers carrying a caseload. More likely they are involved with broader macro issues of policies and procedures, budgeting, forecasting, staff development, regulatory compliance, and the like. This is entirely appropriate, but one downside is that they are no longer direct consumers of the legal services being rendered by outside counsel.

You only get this information if your staff shares concerns that they have. Those concerns may involve late reporting, lack of responsiveness, excessive billings, poor judgment in tactical decisions relating to a case, or failure to follow directions. Make sure your staff is aware that they should alert you to such problems.

Settle!

Do not overlook one obvious option: settle the case. If you are entering a legal battle with weak weapons, you may want and need to take another look at settling the case. Yes, you may have to change your valuation. You may have to pay more. You may have to pay a premium in order to get the case settled.

If the exposure is nasty or the case goes sour, you may be better off settling. If you are exposed to an insured griping that you were negligent in selecting defense counsel, you may need to swallow your pride (and a few dollars) to get the case settled. Hopefully, you are in a position where you just need to pay a little extra to avert trial. The problem comes not when you have to pay just a little more but a whole lot more. Then, the decision becomes more agonizing. What if you are millions of dollars apart?

Pointers from the Field

What if your lawyer experiences something extreme, like a nervous breakdown during trial or on its eve? Barry Zalma, an insurance attorney from Culver City, California, says,

> I would try to never get into such a situation by closer evaluation of the case and counsel. But if I did, counsel's disability would be sufficient for the court to declare a mistrial and order the trial started over just as it would if counsel died in the middle of the trial.

> If the court will not order a mistrial, the second-seat lawyer will have to finish. If there were no second-seat, I'd bring in the meanest barrister-type lawyer I know and pay double his fee to have him move in and try the case.

> More frightening is the situation where you sit through voir dire and opening statement and realize counsel is incompetent and will lose a good case. You must immediately fire him and replace him with a real trial lawyer.

Ken Brownlee, a former corporate risk manager with a global third-party claims administrator and current claims consultant from Georgia recalls,

> I went through a couple of similar situations as risk manager... The breakdown scenario is less likely than what happened at least twice in our trials—the pregnant defense counsel either gave birth early or had a medical crisis!

> Textbook guys usually suggest that for good litigation management we select the attorney and not the firm. Nevertheless, this is where knowing the law firm is as important as knowing the individual defense counsel. In most cases the defense firm acts as a team, with the selected counsel as captain. The best attorney in the worst firm may not be as good a choice as the worst attorney in the best firm if a case is going to go to trial.

Second—make sure you know the law firm's E&O carrier. If you see things starting to fall apart, get the carrier involved very quickly. We had this exact scenario in a products case one time when the defense firm we were managing fell apart (the partners separated, and things went to hell in about a week). Our client and its insured, through us, quickly retained alternate counsel, who settled the case that the insured was certain could have been won at trial. Then they turned to us for what they felt was the difference in settlement versus victory value as an E&O, and we went after the law firm's E&O insurance.

Jack Jensen, cofounder of UltimateInsuranceJobs.com and its vice president of operations, Indianapolis, Indiana, says,

Lean on the principles set in place by the legal infrastructure of the company: internal or external. Is your strongest attorney internal or external? If internal, an appropriate alert should be set in motion to protect the company on other present and future litigious engagements that he would be relied upon to address.

In either case, there should be a sufficient system in place that this attorney reports through on such serious cases. If internal, you need to bolster his absence with others, approach the judge, ask for a change of counsel, and move on. In an external scenario, the firm you deal with should have sufficient depth to respond.

Beaumont Vance, who is with the risk management department of Sun Microsystems, Denver, Colorado, acknowledges that the scenario beginning this chapter is . . .

A bad situation. More likely, the attorney who felt it was a defensible case suddenly panics, claims that you are going to lose big-time, and asks that you throw money at it. Same basic problem—attorney collapse.

If this is a big case, have a strong junior partner or associate on it. I can't imagine going into a large case (over $500,000) without more than one capable attorney on the case. If you don't, better hope that there is a fast learner in the firm who is free tomorrow.

If not, simply have your attorney feign death and ask the courts for some time.

Lousy Lawyer Prevention Checklist

❑ Allow ample lead time to select counsel.
❑ Conduct thorough due diligence on candidate firms and attorneys.
❑ Meet candidate attorneys.
❑ Get and check references.
❑ Draft, communicate, and enforce reasonable service and billing standards.
❑ Have a backup.
❑ Realize perfection is not realistic in attorney selection.
❑ Make sure that you are not simply killing the messenger.
❑ Keep the insured informed (and preferably on board) about attorney problems or contemplated staffing changes.
❑ Encourage and reinforce good behavior from outside counsel.

Approved Lawyer Panels: Good or Bad?

An aside about attorney panels is in order. Approved panels—which are attorneys an insurer has preapproved for work on its claims—have good and bad features. Good features include the following:

- They simplify the attorney selection process.

- They promote efficiency because you don't have to reinvent the wheel every time you hire counsel.

- They lead to long term relationships with a network of outside legal counsel.

- They create a deliverable you can give to insureds and clients, making a good impression and demonstrating a key part of the available service team.

- They offer convenience for new adjusters who want to know which lawyer or firm to use in specific areas.

The flip side is that approved panels may have the following drawbacks:

- Adjusters may use them as a substitute for objectively assessing a firm's performance.

- Panel counsel may develop a sense of complacency or entitlement because of their approved status.

- Prospective accounts may be turned off when a firm they want is excluded from the panel.

- Administrative time and hassle is needed to update the panel, keep track of current billing rates, and negotiate fee schedules.

- Awkward transitions may arise when an attorney you use from panel-approved firm A jumps ship to work at or create firm B. Does your loyalty lie with the firm or with the moving attorney?

- Time is required to evaluate unsolicited proposals from other firms that want to be on the approved panel.

CHAPTER 11

Surviving Claim Audits and Market Conduct Exams

I'm here from the government— I'm here to help you!

You just got a certified mail notice that the state insurance department will be in your claim office in two days to conduct a market conduct review and audit of claim files.

You have forty-eight hours to get ready.

What will you do?

The Claims Audit

Loved or hated, audits are a periodic fact of life for adjusters and claim operations. While audits may not be much fun, being on the receiving end of a claims audit need not be an ordeal. This chapter provides tips on how to emerge from an audit with high marks.

Get an Advance List of the Files

Find out what file selection method the auditor or client will be using. Most have a list of preselected files. Others may pull them at random. Many auditors will mail a list in advance. The amount of notice will vary, but try to negotiate a reasonable amount of advance notice, say two weeks.

The lead time allows the claims manager or supervisor to locate and pull all files on the audit list. It also gives the claim staff a chance to review the files before the audit and anticipate problems.

Review the Files in Advance

This should be standard procedure, but it is surprising how often claim staffs spend little or no time preparing. Check for rocks in the channel. Can you anticipate particular problems? Do the files contain regular status reports, clear documentation on what was done and when, evaluations, recommendations, and rationales for decisions? Are claim file progress notes in the file? Anticipate soft spots, prepare for areas of likely criticism, and formulate your response.

You can often put some context around a claim problem or situation. Most file reviews include a preaudit interview. Typically, the auditor meets with the adjusters, supervisor, and claims manager. This affords a chance to explain candidly any problems the auditor should expect. Setting expectations is key. For example, you may have recently had unusually high personnel turnover. Show the steps you have taken to correct the problem.

Multivolume files are another source of auditor frustration, especially when the clerical staff retrieves only the first or most recent file jacket. According to Ralph Melito, claims specialist with Prudential Re of Newark, New Jersey, "It's frustrating, since your time on-site is limited and you spend some of it doing clerical tasks like hunting down files."

Moral: Make sure all volumes of *each* requested file are available.

Do Some Housecleaning

Like anyone else, auditors develop first impressions. If they open a file and it hemorrhages loose paper and drafts, they may not care how well the adjuster handled the case substantively. They are apt to view everything in a negative light. Remember the old adage, "You only get one chance to make a first impression." It's true! Tidy up. Organize file contents. Put loose paper under brads. Make each file user-friendly. This makes a better impression on the auditor and points to an organized and detail-oriented claims office. This does *not* mean get out the paper-shredder. It means tidying up the files, getting them organized and user friendly, and getting rid of duplicate correspondence in the file.

Have a Preaudit Discussion to Preempt Problems

Seek to lower the auditors' expectations. Meet with them beforehand. If they do not request a preaudit discussion, take the initiative and schedule one anyway. Outline the types of problems they are likely to see. If appropriate, explain the reasons behind the problems. Most auditors will appreciate the candor. They will likely react better than if you boast, "Our files are in great shape!" If you set lower expectations, the auditors are less likely to rake you over the coals. It is human nature to want to see those with hubris taken down a notch. It's no different when it comes to claim audits. An attitude of modesty and candor is more becoming than one of conceit and evasiveness.

Make sure you explain your claims philosophy to the auditor. This may preempt problems. For example, if reserves factor in liability and the auditor assumes you reserve to injury exposure, the auditor may feel you are under-reserving. Setting the ground rules up-front avoids problems.

Prepare the Playing Field

Start right off with an appearance of preparedness and professionalism by having the files ready in a conference room. Key members of the claim staff should be available to answer questions and address concerns. Make sure your key account adjuster is not on vacation or on temporary storm duty.

Any claim operation is busy. An audit is an unwelcome distraction. Each hour devoted to the audit is one hour robbed from actually servicing claim files and clients. Nevertheless, the claims manager—and claim staff— must carve out time. A claims audit is like a final exam. Moral for claim managers: study for your finals!

Pru Re's Ralph Melito suggests other ways that claim departments can make the auditor's life easier:

- Have on hand a copy of the claim department's organizational chart;

- Prepare short biographies of the key account adjusters; and

- Have technical or support staff persons readily available. Some questions may arise that do not warrant interrupting the claims manager, but which a claim technician could easily address.

Show an Interest

If you're a manager, poke your head in the door periodically to ask, "How's it going? Are there any questions I can help with?" This does not mean being intrusive, nosy, or meddlesome. Give the auditors enough space and breathing room to do their job. There is a happy medium between being disinterested and being meddlesome. However, some problems, questions, and misunderstandings can be addressed on the spot and may thereby not make their way into the final written report if you can defuse them verbally. This is not always the case, but there is no harm in trying.

Prepare to Acknowledge Constructive Criticism

Don't react like a hothead to criticism. Listen attentively and admit if you've got problems. If investigations have been lagging, for whatever reason, admit it. If neophyte adjusters are under-reserving, acknowledge the problem. Candor is usually disarming. Even if you strongly disagree with the audit findings, allow some time to cool down before fashioning a response. You will not win a debate with the auditors on-site. (You may not win one after the audit, either!) If anything, you may make them even more entrenched in their positions. View any audit as a way of getting an outsider's view of the claim operation and an opportunity for improvement.

Challenge Faulty Findings

If you disagree with the audit report, you may have a chance to go on record with your rebuttal. It enhances the rebuttal's credibility if the manager can concede certain valid points of criticism. The claims manager may thus have a chance to get in the last word. Like other professionals, auditors have their own biases, preconceptions, background, and competency levels. Anyone can call himself an auditor, and no uniform qualifications exist. Some are first-rate and some are subpar. If the audit findings are flawed, you owe it to yourself, your staff, and the party that commissioned the audit to set matters straight for the record.

Pay Attention to the Obvious

Don't overlook the obvious. The best way to emerge unscathed from an audit is to have the claim files in good shape, including information on prompt and thorough investigations, timely and meaningful reports, realistic reserves, and sufficient file documentation so that the files really *do* speak for themselves.

Periodic self-auditing is a good safeguard against complacency. Whether this means that supervisors read files twice a month or that every file receives a quarterly audit, claim staffs need a systematic way to make sure they follow their own guidelines and adhere to generally accepted adjusting principles.

Because of the negative connotations of the word *audit*, there are signs that at least some of the industry is moving away from the term. The word audit is ominous and evokes an image of someone invading your office to assemble a list of all the things you've done wrong. Because of this, some companies now call the exercises file reviews. The change is more than semantic, since in truth most auditors are not coming into a claims office trying to make adjusters look bad.

Called by whatever name, audits are not fun, but they are an essential exercise for any claim staff. Using these ideas, claim departments can turn the sometimes onerous process into an opportunity to learn ways to improve and deliver superior claim service.

Market Conduct Coping Steps

Here are some ways to avoid a market conduct claims examination.

Utilize In-house or Outside Counsel

Have in-house counsel review all major claim documents. This might include items such as your Claims Manual; litigation guidelines you give to outside defense counsel; and other claims-related brochures, booklets, and promotional material. See whether it poses any problems from a market conduct standpoint. Does it make implicit or explicit promises that may be hard to keep? Does it make any promises that go beyond the insurance policy wording, creating new reasonable expectations in the insured's mind? One example of this would be a statement such as "We communicate with our policyholders before undertaking any action on a claim."

Make sure that manuals and promotional verbiage (including but not limited to your corporate Web site) do not go overboard in making promises (or implied warranties) that can raise consumer expectations or come back to haunt you.

If you have in-house legal counsel and/or a regulatory department, take advantage of them. Be proactive. Don't wait to get to them only after you receive notice of a market conduct survey. The more you invest in getting their views before a crisis, the lower the odds of having a crisis. Consider it preventive medicine for the claims department.

If you do not have in-house counsel or if you cannot get help from your regulatory department, consider seeking help from an outside attorney with experience in insurance regulation and market conduct issues.

In other words, the more time and attention you devote to market conduct issues before a crisis the less likely that you will need to address these in the context of a fine, penalty, visit, or market conduct audit.

Do Not Let Disputed Audit Findings Go Unchallenged

If you disagree with audit findings, dispute them. Of course, do not lose credibility by defending the indefensible. However, if you feel the audit findings are in any way inaccurate, go on record as quickly as possible in explaining your case, point by point. Give this a high priority. Set straight any mistakes or misconceptions.

For example, I worked for an industry captive. We had a fronted program with paper from a major commercial insurer, but our captive reinsured 100 percent of the first $2 million of loss. The captive program had about 500 policyholders. While we were just the reinsurer, most of the claims money was ultimately ours. As a result, we did the front-line claims handling and management. The fronting carrier conducted periodic claim audits. No problem there. The problem was in some post-audit reports in which the auditors referred to the captive reinsurer as *the insured.* This was more than a semantic issue; we felt it implied that there was too cozy a relationship between the policyholders and the claims-handling entity.

This was a key point to correct. The reinsurer was just that—and saw itself as having full independence of claims judgment. It took time to break the auditors of the habit, and for a while the audit reports seemed to group the reinsurer with the policyholders, referring to all as "the insured." (If anything, the fronting carrier, as the ceding company, would be considered "the insured" of my company.)

View the Audit as a Learning Experience

Take the medicine. Distill the audit findings and recommendations into action items that you can use as a blueprint for improvement.

What Is a Market Conduct Examination?

A market conduct examination of an insurance company is a systematic, comprehensive review of all facets of an insurer's business operations in its dealings with customers, consumers, and claimants. The areas subject to review are: (i) company operations and management; (ii) complaint administration; (iii) marketing and sales; (iv) producer (agent) licensing; (v) policyholder service; (vi) underwriting and rating; and (vii) claims administration.

Examiners are either employees of the state insurance department or contract examiners. Examinees must bear the reasonable costs of the examination, which may require up to six months of examiner time (usually two to three individuals).

The repercussions of a poorly managed examination may extend far beyond severe administrative fines and penalties, to include devastating adverse publicity, protracted class action litigation, impairment to competitive advantages, loss of market share, and deterioration of the value of an insurer's operation.

Managing the Process

The good news is that the examination process can be successfully managed. You should strive to:

- Identify the rules, standards, and procedures employed by market conduct examiners,

- Protect confidential and proprietary information,

- Identify the factors that lead regulators to specifically single out an insurer,

- Provide guidance during the examination process to eliminate issues and reduce fines and penalties, and

- Set out procedures and protocols to avoid adverse examinations moving forward.

Determine Reason for Examination

It also helps to determine—preferably in advance—the reason why you are undergoing a market conduct examination. For example,

- Is it a random exam and your company came up?

- Is it in response to consumer or policyholder complaints?

- Is it an across-the-board market conduct exam, in which the examiners will be poking and prodding all functional areas, not just claims?

- Has it been years since the insurance department conducted a survey, so it's time to do one again?

Determine the context in which any market conduct exam will occur. The best situation is when the market conduct exam is a routine exercise. The worst situation is when you have hit the insurance department's radar screen due to consumer or policyholder complaints. Regardless of the situation or the context, take these exercises seriously. If the state insurance department finds that there are market conduct violations, they can assess fines, penalties, and, in extreme cases, suspend one's license to write insurance in the state.

Recognize Areas of Extreme Importance

Know the signs that market conduct examiners look for and avoid tripping up in these areas. Prime market conduct hot spots include the following:

- Misrepresenting pertinent facts or insurance policy provisions regarding the coverage or policy at issue

- Failing to acknowledge and act with reasonable promptness on communications from a policyholder about a claim

- Failing to adopt and implement reasonable standards for prompt claim investigation

- Refusing to pay a claim without conducting a reasonable investigation based on all available information

- Failing to confirm or deny coverage within a reasonable time frame and to provide a reasonable explanation based on information in the policy on why the insurer is denying a claim

- Failing to act in good faith to effectuate prompt, fair, and equitable settlement of claims after liability becomes reasonably clear

- Failing to promptly settle claims when liability under one portion of a policy is reasonably clear in order to influence a settlement under another portion(s) of the coverage

Action Items to Prevent Market Conduct Problems

1. Be meticulous and accurate in representing insurance policy provisions. Quote actual policy language. Minimize interpretation. Make sure that any interpretation is supported by review from outside coverage counsel, if possible.

2. Respond to policyholder communication promptly. Acknowledge immediately. Strive to reply that same

day or within twenty-four hours of receipt. This applies to all types of policyholder communication: mail, fax, or email.

3. Investigate all claims promptly. Set realistic standards for investigations. If factors beyond your control delay the start of an investigation, certain components of it, or its completion, document them thoroughly in the claim file. If the insured's actions in any way have delayed or frustrated the investigation, make a paper trail in the claim file to document.

4. If you deny a claim, make sure that you have investigated it as thoroughly as possible. If the investigation has gaps due to factors beyond your control, note these carefully in the claim file. When denying any claim, close by inviting the insured to provide you with any facts, evidence, or materials that might shed new light on the situation or that might alter your decision.

5. Embrace and enforce rigorous claim service standards.

6. Set/enforce standards that exceed statutory requirements.

7. Be familiar with statutory good faith claim-handling standards. Educate your staff. Spread the word.

8. Treat each consumer complaint promptly and seriously.

9. Treat any insurance department call, letter, or inquiry seriously. Respond rapidly, thoroughly, and nondefensively.

10. Cultivate a good relationship with state insurance departments.

11. Stay off the radar screens of these same insurance departments.

12. Determine if the audit is routine and calendared or if it stems from specific concerns or complaints.

13. Conduct mock-up and internal audits periodically.

CHAPTER 12

Be Careful What You Wish for . . .

Your company may get that
huge account

Your company is fighting hard for the XYZ account. Maybe it looks like a great new chunk of business to the marketing people—a huge company and a flagship account to tout to the public, your competitors, and your peers.

Still, your feelings are a bit conflicted regarding this potential new business. To win the account would be a definite feather in your professional cap. It would provide a needed infusion of new business for your company.

On the other hand, four of your top competitors are also bidding on the business, and there is a chance that one of them will land it. Deep down, you know that winning the account could overtax the capabilities of your existing claim operation.

Secretly, you will be relieved if this great account picks some other company. Of course, the marketing folks don't think that way but, hey, then again they won't be sticking around to service the business. They'll be off pitching the next account, telling them how you and other members of your claims team walks on water. It's your job to live up to such advance billing.

You may win the account and have an influx of new claims that you're not equipped to service.

If you were to win the account, would it be a Pyrrhic victory? How will you ever handle all the extra work with the existing claims staff?

Claims people working with independent adjusting outfits or third-party claim administrators (TPAs) can relate to this. While insurance companies want as few claim assignments as possible, just the opposite is true with TPAs and independent adjusters. If they get paid by the claim, their tendency is to want as many claims as possible. We must therefore distinguish between these outlooks and vast differences in how insurance company claim departments and TPAs view the phenomenon of claim volume. High volume is a bane to insurers but a boon to independent adjusters.

In hurricane prone areas, residents have protocols and procedures about what to do in case of a storm's imminent landfall. They grab duct tape and board up windows. They anchor boats, lawn equipment, and large objects. They draw water and stock emergency supplies. They may leave the area (not an option for the dedicated adjuster) or they may stay and hunker down. Residents would love to have more time and notice to get ready, but often that is not realistic.

Similarly, the claims operation that has won a new account with lots of claims must prepare with the same sense of urgency but not panic. The claims operation is—in a figurative and sometimes in a literal sense—in the eye of the hurricane. Every minute preceding the actual takeover of a new mega-account should be focused on getting ready.

Admittedly, this is a nice problem to have. Many TPAs would kill for this kind of problem. For some, however, the larger challenge lies in increasing business volume.

TPAs typically bid on servicing contracts. These may be for handling claims of either insurance companies or self-insureds. They seek a steady stream of claims to establish a steady source of billings, income, and profit. Sometimes the bids are to handle new claims only. In other cases, the bid might also include assuming existing open or runoff cases. In the latter situation, winning bidders may inherit a large block of existing claims.

If the volume of runoff cases (or even new cases) exceeds a certain level, it can overwhelm the ability of the TPA or independent adjuster to adequately service the account. Often, executives or higher-ups who are not tasked with servicing the business on which they are bidding negotiate the bids. (**Tip:** Encourage the marketing people to consider staffing constraints and have a Plan B in mind to execute or suggest if the company ends up winning the business.) This difference in perspective is important. If the floodgates open and the claims operation is not set up to digest it, various adverse consequences can flow, such as:

- degraded service to the new client

- complaints from claimants

- degraded service to existing clients

- organizational and workload stresses on claim staff, with plummeting morale and productivity

- adjuster staff attrition and turnover

Burning the Midnight Oil

When this situation confronted one seasoned claims professional, his response was "I just work twenty-hour days." That strategy might last a while, but at some point the adjusting machinery breaks down. You cannot do a good job investigating, negotiating, or analyzing if you're burnt out from overwork or fatigue. Mistakes occur. Good people wear out and quit. Everyone is miserable. It is not a recipe conducive to having the claims operation shine.

A Challenge from the Field

I recall an early career experience with a national TPA. The company had just won the workers compensation claim-service contract for a large municipal transit system. This included handling all on-the-job injuries from employees who operated and serviced buses and subways. The municipality had about 8,000 employees and 3,000 open workers compensation claims when we took over the account.

In fact, the municipality—in its prior self-administration days—put injured bus drivers to work at temporary or modified duty jobs handling workers compensation claims. Many claims were paid on dubious grounds. Former bus drivers functioned as newly appointed claims handlers, sitting in judgment of the benefit eligibility for their peers and good buddies. As one can imagine, this was a recipe for claim disaster.

Everyone seemed to feed at the workers compensation trough. The transit authority's former risk manager was on a permanent total award for psychological disability. An in-house attorney filed for a back injury she claimed she suffered in her condo one weekend while bending over to review a (literally) heavy workers compensation file she had taken home. No wonder the claim volume was high.

When we won the account, the moving vans literally backed up to the dock at the base of our office building and unloaded about 250 boxes of workers compensation claim files. Now the real fun began.

Dozens of adjusters worked almost around the clock, coding the cases, setting them up, and entering the information into the company's claim database. Temps were hired. Midnight oil was burned on weekdays and weekends. Eventually, the claims office worked the files down to a fraction of open cases, but the cost was a high degree of adjuster attrition and turnover. Many just could not or would not take the pressure. Some very good claims people quit and went to work for competitors. We hired three claims people from the TPA that had previously handled the account. Within a few months, all three were gone.

Get As Much Lead Time As Possible

The more time you have to prepare the better. If you can negotiate the takeover date, do so to buy yourself preparation time. Use this time to get ready: staff up, lease extra space, order additional workstations and computers, and develop training and orientation materials on the new account. Make sure that the client knows that you're doing this—not to delay—but to gear up to do the best job possible. In the long run, the client will benefit. Despite best efforts, however, there will be situations in which you simply will have deadlines forced on you.

Hire Temps

Keep the names of local, regional, or national adjuster temporary staffing agencies available. In addition, many insurance placement specialists have the resumes of claims people who are between jobs or who are permanent temps. Some claims people have found a rewarding career niche in temping because they want flexibility in when, where, and how long they work. Temps can be the shock troops thrown into the breach.

The sooner you can get a temp to supplement permanent staffers the better. The drawback of the temp is the cost, although there may be offsetting economies. For example, you may not have to pay benefits to temporary workers.

Some staffing agencies even offer a type of lease with an option to buy. That is, if the temp works out, you may want to hire her. Perhaps you can transition this person into a permanent employee.

Tips on Temps

Check credentials. A seasoned property insurance adjuster may do you little good if you are taking over a large number of auto accident claims

Verify licensing. Some states and jurisdictions are finicky about making sure that claim handlers are current in their licenses. Check to see if your state falls into this category.

Negotiate price. Temps are not cheap. But bear in mind that in the area of temps—as in other realms—you get what you pay for. Nevertheless, this is a competitive business. Parlay that to your advantage.

Delegate the job of hiring. Assign a capable staff person to this task. Your time may be better spent gearing up for the new influx of claims.

Hire. If they work out, consider offering them permanent full-time positions. In fact, some temp agencies discount their fees if you end up hiring one of their representatives.

Other Options

Hire More Staff

Temps are, well, temps. By definition, they are stopgap, short term, and temporary employees. Temps are expensive and may not be long-run solutions to staffing shortfalls. The longer-term solution is to get permanent employees in to service the new claims.

Compose Job Descriptions for the New Positions

In fact, it helps to have job descriptions written out in advance. This gets you out of the starting blocks quickly whenever you have to reenter the job market, trolling for claims talent. Keep the job descriptions and ads current. Put them on a word processor so that you can update and revise very quickly.

Seek help from corporate or from other branches. Get the word out that this is your moment of need.

Don't Forget the Rest of Your Business

It's critical to remember that, even though the new account is very important, it's still only one account for which you are responsible. It's no good to lose a long-standing client because of neglect in the fact of a new one.

Nancy Germond of The Insurance Writer, Jefferson City, Missouri, suggests,

> Hire some retired adjusters who want to make a few bucks and have forgotten more about claims than we remember to help overview the claims, synopsize them, and make suggestions. It's really important to immediately meet with the new account to see what their expectations are in handling, too. And do not bad mouth the old TPA. That's a no-no. It's tempting, though.

Karen Ali, customer account manager for Acordia of West Virginia reasons,

> I worked for a company that had just received a contract to administer the workers compensation claims of a large hospital chain that had entered financial difficulty. We were to handle workers compensation claims established prior to the bankruptcy. I was brought in to clean up the backlog of unpaid bills and bring order out of chaos. The week prior to my placement there, the company had received approximately ninety large cartons of paper files for these claims. To say it was a mess is an understatement!

One important thing is to organize, organize, organize. Once I got the boxes of files into an order where I could find what I needed when I needed it, things began to flow. By organizing files, I got familiar with the claimants, their claim issues, injuries, prior treatments, etc. Of course, I had timelines that had to be met in handling bill payments, but it all worked together. I waded through bills and organized them into an alpha order system. By this time, we had received a printout from the employer of the bills that had been paid on claims up to the point of bankruptcy. This helped in doing matchups.

Don't Bid without Having the Resources Marshaled

Dave Morgan of Morgan Bishop Company (United Kingdom) has faced this problem a number of times over the years. He reiterates the need to prepare to take over a large account.

My game was employer's liability and, with that class, there's usually a delay between winning the account and starting to see the claims.

However, with the larger accounts we always looked into claims resources to see whether we would be able to service the account, and the more enlightened brokers and/or clients do as well. I have won accounts before on my ability to service volumes of claims that the competition would not have been able to handle. I have also refused to quote for a couple of accounts because I knew the volume of claims could not be handled with the resources we had.

It's not really rocket science if you think it through, but a good number of insurers don't think about it and concentrate more on the income when quoting for business.

Out of interest, I've also seen an account that produced a large number of attritional claims put on the books purely to justify a particular number of staff in the claims department. Although that account lost money technically, it did mean that the claims department had enough staff to provide good service to all of our customers, so it was actually a good move.

Alert Underwriting

If you are an insurance company claims person and you see a big influx of claims without a corresponding increase in accounts, talk to the underwriting department. Do this as early as possible and in advance of any upcoming renewal. The uptick in loss reporting may be a material underwriting factor in the account's attractiveness and renewability. Avoid a situation in which you get around to alerting underwriting ten days after it has renewed the account. Perhaps your employer needs to get off the account as soon as possible because the loss influx may herald an incipient claims meltdown.

There is a school of thought in insurance that frequency precedes severity. To that extent, an upswing in loss or claim reporting is a key piece of advance information that you should give to the underwriter. Confirm your conversation with a memo or email. (Keep a copy for when the boss sees the big claim numbers and asks, "What's going on with the claims?!") Be vocal, be proactive, and don't worry about coming across as Chicken Little. Part of your job is to provide an effective feedback loop with the folks who select and price the risks.

Preventive Checklist

New Account Overload: Six Steps to Avoid Crises

1. Make sure the marketing people know your capabilities and resource needs in advance of quoting on new business.

2. Just say no. Don't be afraid to say no thanks to bidding on business opportunities that you know will outstrip your ability to provide competent service. A no may cause short-term heartburn but avert long-term heartache. As Dirty Harry Callahan said, "A man's got to know his limitations." Good advice for a claims operation, too!

3. Have back-up staffing contingency plans ready in case you land a new account.

4. Cultivate good relations with adjuster staffing services and keep resumes on hand of candidates that you might need down the road.

5. Maintain contact with one or more skilled office-leasing agents who can rapidly find you additional office space or equipment at competitive rates in case you need to expand operations.

6. Keep tabs on TPA services that can assist on an overflow basis.

CHAPTER 13

When Disaster Strikes

Dealing with a catastrophe

Your area just got hit with a disaster and must keep operating even though your offices are damaged. Police have cordoned off your street, so you can't get to your building. Your adjusters are scattered, making it a challenge getting through to them.

What will you do?

Claims Department Disaster Planning

Adjusters and claim professionals face unique challenges in preparing for disasters. At these times, they are expected to be at the top of their game. The disaster could be an earthquake or a tornado, or it could involve the claims office being in an area hit by a hurricane. Maybe it is in an area laid low by a severe blizzard, ice storm, or flood. Mother Nature has a wide variety of challenges to throw at claims operations.

Not all the perils are acts of nature, though. Consider the challenges of running a claims office in lower Manhattan on September 11, 2001. One affected claims manager confided to me, "I was never trained as a crisis counselor, but I had to become one pretty fast."

In these situations, claim operations are not like most other businesses. A gas station can close. The shopping mall may opt to shutter its storefronts. Claim operations cannot snuggle under the covers and call in sick, though. Like hospitals and firefighters, claim operations have to rise to the challenge. Folks count on them.

People expect the claims unit to be a paragon of preparedness. The challenges are at least two-fold. One is to restore order in the actual claims operation. The other is to focus on external factors and the need to service policyholders and claimants. They don't care that you have been in the same disaster. They are—understandably—focused on their own needs. They figure that disasters are your business, and you've spent your time getting ready. Have you, though? Let's find out.

Preparedness Checklist

Here are six groups of questions that you can use as a checklist to see how well prepared your claims operation is for the next big challenge:

- Do you have a disaster recovery plan? Is it written down? Is your staff familiar with it? Do you periodically practice your disaster recovery plan? Do you take it seriously or view it as one thing to cross off the checklist to appease the Home Office? A commitment to disaster recovery planning must be more than a checklist or pro forma item. Read, review, and brush up on it.

- Are your computer files backed up? How frequently? Where is the backup media stored? (Hopefully, offsite in a far away location!) If your claims office were destroyed, could you reconstruct missing claim files? How and how long would it take? Many claim operations are only as good as their databases and their IT infrastructure. How impregnable is yours?

- If disaster were to strike, what would you do for alternative or temporary office space?

- Do you have a way to contact all of your employees in an emergency? Do you have home phone and cell phone numbers? Email addresses?

- If you needed a mass infusion of catastrophic adjusters due to a local calamity, where would you go? How about administrative and support staff? Do you have ties to a temp agency that you can summon in a pinch?

- Do you know the critical functions necessary to keep your claims department up and running?

Tip

Gather all the home phone numbers, cell phone numbers, and home/personal email addresses of all the claims staff. Let the staff know that you are not playing Big Brother—you just want to be able to contact them in case of an emergency. Make duplicate copies and store the list at multiple offsite locations. Make sure that claim managers and supervisors have a copy. In case of an emergency, having this list will make it easier to communicate to your claims staff about office openings, meeting points, assignments, and other procedures for responding to the catastrophe.

> ## Tip
>
> Stock your office with some disaster basics. This might include five-gallon jugs of water, energy bars, first aid kits, battery-powered radios, emergency/space blankets, flashlights, and candles. (Some might suggest duct tape and plastic sheeting as well, given periodic upgrades in terrorism alert levels.) Give some thought to what your claims operation would do in the event of a disaster that occurred during work hours.

Tom Pickhardt, CPCU, director, Insurance Division of Attus Technologies, Inc., in Charlotte, North Carolina, states

> I was at [a major insurer's] office [recently] and know that they have a very serious initiative underway to get disaster kits out to all their offices. Their conference room was full of boxes of walkie-talkies, shoulder bags, and other assorted items.

If electronic communications are still intact, harness the Internet to enhance disaster response and communication. Brady Smith, product development specialist at Mutual of Enumclaw, Madison, Wisconsin states,

> The Internet can be a real asset in claims handling. After major windstorms in our area, power and phone lines were down. Cell phone circuits were overloaded. If you were lucky to find a working phone, calling a claims office got you a continuous busy signal. If you had a claim, you were out of luck until the line cleared. Many people could make it to an office and had PCs, though. An insurer with a Web site claims form would have a leg-up on customer service in receiving claims and communicating with its adjusters, making full use of the Internet's design specifications (communicating when normal communications are disrupted) to help people needing assistance.

Claim professionals can't expect to have an effective disaster recovery response without putting plans to the test in practice. Another terrorist act or natural disaster is no time to be dusting off the plan, trying to remember who does what.

Let's look at one example, not from the claims industry but still from the financial services sector. Shortly after the first plane hit on September 11th at the World Trade Center, the evacuation of Morgan Stanley employees was so calm and orderly that you might've thought that they'd done it all before.

In fact, they had. They weren't content with just designing an evacuation plan. They rehearsed it in case the need ever arose. It did—on September 11th.

This offers an instructive lesson for claim professionals. The more we sweat by practicing a disaster recovery plan, the less we bleed when the real deal appears in the form of a catastrophic loss. Drill, drill, and then drill some more. Do it until it is second nature.

After recent national security alerts regarding possible terrorist attack, individuals flooded home improvement stores, stocking up on items like duct tape and plastic sheeting, along with bottled water, manual can openers, and other survival goods. Not a bad idea. Has your claim office taken heed of this? If not, think through what you might need in the event of a disaster. True, nothing is foolproof and you may not know until it's too late whether you've done enough.

Do not, however, succumb to a sense of fatalism that "If it happens, there's nothing we can do." Survival favors the prepared, so boost your odds by planning ahead. Disaster recovery planning is no longer just a theoretical exercise for claim operations. It is not just a nice concept to preach to policyholders for whom you or your company writes business interruption coverage. Get serious about disaster recovery planning and make sure that your claims operation is a model of preparedness.

Get Ready

If and when disaster strikes, the demands and expectations imposed on claim departments will increase, not decrease. In this regard, claim operations differ from most other businesses, where consumers may be willing to cut some slack. The bar is raised for claim operations in these situations.

Barry Zalma, an insurance attorney from Culver City, California, says that in the event of a disaster,

> I'd get up off the floor, make sure my family was safe and taken care of, and then try to contact my employees. I'd find some place to replace my office, rent a motor home or trailer. I'd establish immediate communication—cell phones, telephones. Finally, I would sit down, cry, and get back to work. Of course, if I was really smart, I would have been prepared with a portable office in a secure place, a backup of all my files and records, with cellular communications, food, and water.

Resources for Preparing Your Claims Operation

There are a number of books on organization disaster planning. Two of them are *Business at Risk: How to Assess, Mitigate, and Respond to Terrorist Threats* (National Underwriter Company, 2002) and *Emergency Preparedness for Facilities,* (Casavant Publishing, 2003). They can help you create organization-wide emergency management plans that ensure that prudent procedures are in place and that equipment and personnel needs are addressed so you can respond to an emergency situation quickly and instinctively. They help you maximize the odds that you and your adjusters are trained and prepared to put a plan into action and protect workers, property, and the life of the company in the face of an emergency event— whether natural or manmade.

The books identify and examine natural and nonnatural emergencies, defined as anything that disrupts an organization, including:

- power outages

- chemical spills

- bomb threats

- riots or demonstrations

- workplace violence

- fires

- droughts

- blizzards

- floods

- terrorist actions

Claim operations deal in the business of loss and risk. Customers, clients, and members of the public expect an extra level of preparedness from them. They cannot be (or at least should not be) like the proverbial cobbler's kids, running around barefoot. Charity—and good risk management—begins at home.

Establish contingency plans with another local business for use of its facilities until you can resume claim-handling operations on your own well in advance of any catastrophe. Computer data backups should have already been in place and housed off site.

There should also be plans for temporary staff to arrive from out of the area, as local staff will obviously be busy putting their personal lives back together, and incoming claims resulting from the disaster will need to be handled.

Adjuster Allan Ballow writes,

After Hurricane Hugo in 1989, the barrier island (Isle of Palms, South Carolina) where I live was cut off from the mainland for days—no power, no phones, water, etc. Roads were impassable, blocked by downed trees, houses, boats, and so on. *Nationwide Insurance* adjustors were here with laptops, mopeds, and checkbooks. This so impressed me I moved my house and car coverage to Nationwide. Mobile technology has only improved since then so the response today should be even better, *if an insurer wants to do it rather than make excuses*. I know this is just anecdotal, but it was very impressive from the insured's point of view.

Note how a claims operation response in times of emergency and disaster can have a huge marketing payoff. The ability to respond quickly under trying circumstances may provide more marketing punch than a glossy magazine ad or TV campaign. Insureds may be so impressed by a claims operation's ability to respond in the clutch that customers may look for ways to migrate other lines of coverage over to the insurer that is able to respond.

Part of the claims department's mission is not only to take care of its customers but to take care of its employees as well. One way to do this is through the use of an employee assistance plan.

Install an Employee Assistance Program (or Publicize the One You Have)

If your company does not have an employee assistance program (EAP), consider adding one to your menu of benefits. If you do have an EAP, be sure to remind your employees of the fact and encourage them to utilize it. Some employees bear up under stress better than others. With an EAP, the employer gives workers the name and number of an outside service they can call for help on problems that don't fit neatly into any occupational cause.

The EAP may provide counseling or referral to other resources. More and more workers have come to expect an EAP as part of a competitive benefits package. Structured thoughtfully, employee assistance programs can be effective crisis management and coping tools. Merely having an EAP, though, is no guarantee that the program delivers this type of payback.

Publicize the EAP, stressing its confidential nature. Adjusters in stricken areas must not only deal with their own stress, but they also must deal with the needs and demands of stressed out claimants and insureds. This may create a pressure cooker environment for claim managers and supervisors. EAPs often provide telephone counselors twenty-four-hours a day. Here is what some companies do to manage employee stress in difficult times:

- J. Walter Thompson gave employees booklets, home mailings, and email with information on the EAP, letting them know that counselors were available. The communications also described emergency procedures such as evacuation plans.

• Fannie Mae, the Washington, D.C., area mortgage lender, posted emergency information and other data regarding its EAP on its employee's Intranet site.

• Allstate Insurance Company puts stress management tips on its Intranet site, encouraging employees to maintain routines and to avoid heated workplace discussions on politics or war.

(From "On Home Front, Businesses Try to Ease Staffs' Stress," *USA Today*, 3/24/03, p. B2.)

Sample Disaster Recovery Plan

Purpose: The purpose of this emergency plan is to cover emergency situations that would prevent access to our corporate computer or business facilities at [INSERT ADDRESS]. Were this to occur, the company would declare a corporate-wide emergency and would establish temporary processing facilities to ensure access to needed corporate/department claims data, files, and corporate communications.

Declaring an Emergency: Unless the XYZ Company corporate facilities are in a quarantined area (due to natural or manmade disaster), the facilities will be inspected by a member of the Crisis Team or corporate officer as soon as possible after a disaster occurs. If the company determines that an emergency must be declared, a corporate officer or representative (from a designated list) must declare an emergency and:

1. Contact ABC vendor to reserve off-site claim processing facilities.
2. Contact the XYZ Company crisis team. The crisis team will meet at the [INSERT NAME AND ADDRESS OF LOCAL HOTEL OR MOTEL] or another site to be determined at the time of the emergency.
3. Contact all XYZ Company officers (see separate list). Each officer will contact his or her respective staffs.

Note: When an emergency is declared—with the exception of the Crisis Team—all XYZ employees should remain at their homes until contacted by the Crisis Team. If an emergency forces an adjuster to evacuate the area, it is the employee's responsibility to contact a crisis team member with a forwarding telephone number as soon as possible.

Emergency Plan: In the event of an emergency, XYZ Company will

1. Assemble the Crisis Team to coordinate the emergency. Primary meeting place will be at [INSERT NAME AND ADDRESS OF LOCAL HOTEL/MOTEL].
2. Establish temporary off-site claims processing facility. The facility will initially provide access to claims data and corporate communication for a core team of [insert number] adjusters. XYZ Company will have full backups of all systems at an off-site location.
3. Temporary processing for claims via laptops and cell phones will be established until ABC vendor is operational.

Who can declare an emergency. The following officers or managers can declare an emergency with ABC Vendor:

[Insert names, phone numbers, and cell phone numbers of executives and/or managers.]

XYZ Crisis Management Team. The following personnel are on the first call crisis team:

[Insert names, phone numbers, and cell phone numbers.]

Alternates

[Insert names, phone numbers, and cell phone numbers.]

XYZ Officers Contact List. The following XYZ officers/managers must be called when an emergency is declared:

[Insert names, phone numbers, and cell phone numbers.]